Gretchen

The Windsors I Knew

An American Private Secretary's Memoir
of
the Duke and Duchess of Windsor

NASSAU, BAHAMAS 1940-1944

JEAN D. HARDCASTLE-TAYLOR
EDITED BY HUGO VICKERS

Cover Design by Victoria Gallery and Shari Gallery
VisualVictoria.com
Layout by: Shari Gallery
Cover photo of the Duke and Duchess from a British military
newspaper, *The North Caribbean Star*, Special Bahamian Edition.

ISBN: 978-1-9769307-2-0

"Never marry a man, Miss Drewes, with the idea of changing him."

Advice from the Duchess of Windsor to the author, in a limousine on their way to a cinema in Nassau, 1944

The Duchess of Windsor outside her United Services Canteen, circa 1944.
Source: Author's collection

DEDICATION

The author's children and grandchildren wish to dedicate the author's memoir to the memory of the Duke and Duchess of Windsor. This wartime couple was well aware of difficult economic and social conditions in the Bahamas from their arrival in August 1940, and worked diligently from the start of their official duties as Governor General and First Lady to improve the lot of the people of the colony. They achieved substantial progress. The author witnessed in private the anguish shared by the Duke and Duchess throughout the war and wanted people to know this when she finished her work about 1965.

We also wish to dedicate this memoir to the people of the Bahamas and to the men and women of the British Empire and American armed forces who trained and served in the Bahamas during World War II.

No dedication would be complete without a few words of fond remembrance of a truly amazing and resourceful mother. Highly intelligent and loyal to her royal employers, friends and family, she brought four children into the world in the five years immediately following her service to the Duke and Duchess of Windsor, and provided the finest of shepherding to us all through high school and beyond. She was a wonderful woman and mother!

It seems clear that the special qualities the Duke and Duchess saw in their private secretary while they all worked together in Nassau were the same as those her children benefitted from until her untimely passing in 1970. So this is for you Mom. It is your legacy. May your memories live on!

Michael Hardcastle-Taylor

Eldest son of the author and assembler of her memoir.

INTRODUCTION

Much has been written about the Duke and Duchess of Windsor. Nearly 80 years after the Abdication, historians of varying merit ponder the issue – why did he do it? Was it the greatest love story of the 20th century? Did Mrs. Simpson steal the King? Was he pushed out as a dangerous figure who would attempt to ally Britain to the Nazis in Germany? Was he then a traitor? One book even suggested that Mrs. Simpson was more in love with Mr. Simpson and wished she could have stayed with him, another that she might have been a man. So it goes on.

I have contributed to this debate myself and my conclusion, for what it is worth, is that Edward VIII did not want to be King. There is plenty of evidence that he was bored with his royal duties, that he contemplated escaping to the ranch in Canada with Freda Dudley Ward, and that he longed to give the whole thing up. Unless he was even more removed from reality than at times he appears to be, he must have realized that the British Establishment would never accept as Queen a woman with two husbands living. Surely, if subconsciously, he used Mrs. Simpson as a means of escape.

If that appears somewhat blunt, there is no doubt that he soon realized that he had put her in an intolerable position by turning her into this hated figure. He failed to have her accepted by his family and he failed to get her made a Royal Highness.

Another thought occurs to me, based on examining this story for fifty years. The world loved the Prince of Wales, deeming him to have great charm, but those who knew him and worked for him had serious reservations. On the other hand, the world loathed Mrs. Simpson, but those who knew her and worked for her, respected her and rather liked her. Cecil Beaton, a good judge of character, knew her well. After attending the Duke of Windsor's funeral in 1972, he wrote:

"History will make his love story into a romance. In fact, for us so close, it is hard to see that. Wallis has been a good friend to me, I like her. She is a good friend to all her friends. There is no malice in her. There is nothing dislikeable. She is just not of the degree that has reason to be around the throne."

It seems to me that if ever the choice needs to be made between following the path of duty and the path of perceived happiness, it is best to choose the path of duty. It will make you happier in the long run. I only saw the Duke of Windsor once in my life and I have never seen a man with sadder eyes.

When I was writing *Behind Closed Doors*, I went to a conference in Coronado, across the Bay from San Diego and met Michael Hardcastle-Taylor and his wife Gloria. Mike had a typescript written by his late mother, Jean Drewes, who had worked for the Windsors as their private secretary, in the years during his Governorship of the Bahamas from 1940 to 1944. Here is a vivid account of their day-to-day life, as seen by one working right inside Government House, Nassau. Jean Drewes observed her royal employers with a keen eye.

Those that write about the Windsors today do so, inevitably, second hand. Here we have a vivid first-hand account of what they were like. As such it has value. I was keen to quote from it in my book and Mike allowed me. In turn I have helped, in a small way, to edit the text and I am sure it will be read with great interest in many corners of the world.

Hugo Vickers
August 2015
London

CONTENTS

An Unforgettable Adventure

A girl never knows how her life can suddenly change. Mine changed on a cold November day in 1940 when the executive secretary of Mount Holyoke College Club in New York referred me to an employment agency on Broadway. There I was told, "There is a big job in the offing— three weeks have gone by and it is still unfilled. No information is available except that it is highly confidential and it pays very well. It is outside of the country and your credentials are obviously first-class. Here are the details of whom to contact. Hurry and good luck!" I was directed to an impressive town house just off Fifth Avenue, belonging to Mrs. Kermit Roosevelt.

I was obviously well acquainted with the Roosevelt name, but I did not know much about this particular Mrs. Roosevelt. She turned out to be the daughter-in-law of President Theodore Roosevelt. Her husband was his second son. She had been born as Belle Wyatt Willard in Baltimore. Her father, Joseph E. Willard, owned the Willard Hotel in Washington, and had served as Ambassador to Spain under President Woodrow Wilson. At first I was not told who was seeking to employ me, but it was not Mrs. Roosevelt. She was acting on behalf of a friend.

Her house was nothing if not overwhelming. It was positively buzzing with activity. Mrs. Roosevelt had many interests – including welfare endeavors in the United States, supporting the British war effort, as well as her employment agency. America's entry into the war was still about a year away, but at that particular time she was busy promoting one of the first "Bundles for Britain" ideas. Printed circulars and advertising material were stacked all over the house. Activity was everywhere. One room resembled the mail division of a huge commercial firm. Telephones were ringing. Volunteers and paid helpers were all working hard in a wonderful and commendable war project.

First I was interviewed by Mrs. Roosevelt's personal secretary. Having passed that test, I was ushered into Mrs. Roosevelt's private study, a finely appointed room in paneled oak. She rose from behind her desk and greeted me with a smile. But within minutes she had floored me: "Miss Drewes, you will have to first pronounce my name right! It is Roosevelt (like rose) and not Roooooosevelt!" I apologized profusely; she smiled again and the interview proceeded.

In a few words she outlined that the post was one requiring considerable confidentiality, a most responsible position. I was still bemused and the more so when she announced that my employers were to be the Duke and Duchess of Windsor. I discovered later that

1

Mrs. Roosevelt and the Duchess had both been Baltimore socialites in their youth. The Windsors' previous secretary, Miss Dina Wells Hood, had left from their villa in the South of France on 1 September 1939. They had employed no secretary for the past year since they left France when the Duke took on his appointment as Governor of the Bahamas in August 1940.

To be Governor of the Bahamas would not perhaps have been the Duke's first choice. But the British Government did not want him in England and they did not want him drifting about Europe, where he might well have been captured by the Germans and used as a political prisoner. So it was the obvious solution.

I told Mrs. Roosevelt how pleased I was to have been selected and she followed by stating that I did not have the position yet. I must prove my worth as a private secretary by serving her in that capacity for a day or so before she could recommend me. Furthermore, my credentials were to be thoroughly checked. The following day, I was put through my paces. It was high-powered stuff but I enjoyed the pressure. Mrs. Roosevelt impressed me as being a business dynamo. She was friendly and appreciative of my services. I liked her.

The scrutiny was intense. My personal references were checked and re-checked minutely. My family was deemed to be satisfactory. The fact that I was an alumna of Mount Holyoke College and Katharine Gibbs School for Educated Women was to my credit. My European travels as a college student gave me some international credentials. Furthermore, and of prime importance, they were satisfied that I was a thoroughly experienced secretary. My college friend, Louise Virginia Nunn, who happened to be a personal friend of Mrs. Roosevelt's private secretary, vouched for me wholeheartedly. She had been the buyer of leather goods and notions at R.H. Macy's and later served as placement director of Katharine Gibbs School in New York. Her recommendation carried the necessary weight.

Later I heard from Mr. Kendrick A. Luther, a former Vice President of the Aetna Life Insurance Company, for whom I had worked as secretary, that he had twice been contacted by Mrs. Roosevelt asking about my qualifications. He told me that the dinner guests at his home in Southport, Connecticut, were duly impressed when the butler summoned him from the drawing room to the telephone: "Mrs. Roosevelt is calling *again* from New York … " Then, too, I had taken courses in music, art and interior decoration in my spare time; and, as chairman, I had organized the Junior Woman's Club of Mamaroneck and was an active member of the Community Drama Society in my hometown.

The day after my working session with Mrs. Roosevelt, a cable recommending me was sent to Captain Vyvyan Drury, Equerry to His Royal Highness (HRH) The Duke of Windsor, Government House, Nassau, Bahamas (who during the war was serving the

Governor as Press Liaison Officer). It bore Mrs. Roosevelt's signature. I was offered the job and accepted with a mixture of excitement and trepidation.

I had been staying with my brother and his wife in Mount Vernon, New York. They were soon caught up in the excitement. I only had two days to assemble a southern wardrobe. While I was out shopping, they were suddenly besieged by newspaper reporters who even tried to seize an attractive photograph of my sister-in-law from the baby grand piano in their home and print it, saying it was me. They failed to get it. Reviewing my appointment, my bemused brother could only comment, "It's terrific!"

I was to have flown to Nassau but a blinding blizzard grounded all the southbound air traffic. I quickly booked accommodation by railroad. It was really hectic but finally I was on my way. As the train left New York in the direction of Miami, I was convinced that I had set out on an unforgettable adventure.

Author at Grand Central Station, New York, setting off for Nassau and her "Unforgettable Adventure", December 1940.

FIRST IMPRESSIONS

I arrived in Miami with no further intrusions from journalists and flew from Florida to New Providence Island in a huge amphibian plane. It was a lovely day and the climate was perfect for early December. It was about 80 degrees and humid, a far cry from the blizzard I had left behind in New York. As we approached the Pan American Airways' land base, I saw that the flowers were all in bloom and I said to myself, "I'm going to enjoy this experience." On landing I was greeted by Detective-Sergeant Harry Holder of New Scotland Yard who later observed that he guessed at once that I was the "American secretary" on account of my briefcase and dark glasses.

Government House was being redecorated to suit the Duchess of Windsor's particular taste, so Corporal Sawyer, the second chauffeur, drove me in the station wagon up Bay Street and deposited me at Cumberland House, a guest house down the hill from Government House. I would stay here for a few weeks. Major Gray Phillips, the Comptroller of the Household[1], had left me a note welcoming me to Nassau.

I had just finished a tasty luncheon in the hotel garden under the palm trees when Major Phillips appeared. He was a distinguished-looking gentleman, British from his toes to his impressive height of six feet, three inches. He welcomed me as his future associate and did his best to explain the royal routine. Under his instructions, as a member of the Windsor household, I was to address the Duchess as "Your Royal Highness", by specific instruction of the Duke. He said that the Duke would meet me in the morning in his office and that later I would be introduced to the Duchess. He then departed and I re-read his note of welcome.

So here I was in Nassau, a place long famous for pirates, buried treasure and bootlegging. Bay Street was known as "Booze Avenue" and a paradise for the rich, especially rich Americans. Nassau, with her sapphire sky and billowy clouds and emerald-blue sea, with her floral beauty and fragrance (ignoring the odoriferous fishing docks and adjacent Bay Street area), with her cocoa palms and pink and yellow stucco houses, with her primitive native shacks in contrast to her fine hotels and impressively-appointed clubs, with her golfing, swimming, dancing and horse-racing amenities; Nassau with the charm of

---

[1] Major Gray Phillips was assisted by Captain Vyvyan Drury. Their household staff also included a private secretary (the author), three clerks, a valet, a butler, a French chef, ten servants and Detective Sergeant Harold (Harry) Holder from Scotland Yard, who had been assigned to protect them during their escape from Lisbon. The Duchess's maid was Evelyn Fryth.

her glass-bottomed boats revealing wondrous marine gardens containing anemones, coral formations and sea fans, with her sponge market, with her native ladies casually balancing huge bundles or straw baskets, jammed full, on their heads, with her antiquated, fringe-trimmed carriages drawn by half-starved nags which would bite anyone who unwisely petted their heads, and with her Bay Street shopkeepers completely indifferent as to their daily cash take and the possible depletion of their well-stocked inventories.

Successive American tourist seasons had poured thousands of dollars into their coffers until they were literally bulging at the seams! Nassau, with perfect winter weather, the calm, still sea occasionally contrasted by torrential rains, followed by turbulent and riotous seas; with her lovely Paradise Beach and clear iridescent waters. As they advertised, Old Nassau was a place where "languid tranquility prevails!"

At the appointed hour the next morning, I appeared at the Governor's office, adjacent to Government House proper, closely scrutinized by the two other English Aides-de-Camp. I was ushered into the room, which was plain, typically colonial and a far cry from what I imagined he had been used to at Buckingham Palace. I found myself standing in front of His Royal Highness and my knees literally shook. I was formally presented by Major Phillips and the Duke shook my hand. He soon put me at ease with a friendly smile. He looked me straight in the eyes and gave me his undivided attention.

Rising from a quick and rather amateurish curtsy, I was struck by the intangible and indefinable quality of his presence. This was the erstwhile Prince of Wales, loved by the world, boyish in manner and figure, but enveloped in an invisible armor of royal dignity and invested with unmistakable authority. On second glance, I realized that the Duke looked older than I had expected, yet he was still jaunty, his hair quite blond, his eyes blue and his skin nicely tanned, giving him a healthy glow. He was debonair, likeable and serious. Although small of stature, he possessed a forceful personality. His voice boomed with authority throughout his office and I realized that he literally spoke "the King's English".

His clothes reflected excellent taste. There was a studied casualness about him. He was dressed in a trim, well-cut white linen sports suit. His smart brown and white sports shoes were distinctly British. His blue pastel sport shirt with the famous Windsor collar was set off by his equally renowned widespread plaid Windsor knotted tie.

The Duke invited me to sit down (one never sits in the presence of royalty except by invitation) and immediately started to ply me with innumerable questions as to my trip down to Miami, my flight to Nassau, my first impressions of the Island, my association with Mrs. Roosevelt, my educational and business background.

The Duke appeared slightly nervous at first and fidgety, but somehow my direct

6

answers overcame this. I hope he was reassured to find me an experienced business girl, not wholly overawed by the assignment. He told me that "Her Royal Highness" would be meeting me a little later in the day and then the interview was over. His welcome was so sincere that I was soon convinced that I would enjoy serving both him and his wife.

My meeting with the Duchess was much more informal. She even introduced herself to me, which surprised me. I was in the midst of sorting out the mail under the guidance of Mrs. Greta Moxley (then secretary to Captain Drury), who later acted as my assistant. All of a sudden, there she was before me – The Duchess of Windsor – a veritable picture, as though she had stepped from a page in *Vogue*. She was charming, very lovely and perfectly groomed. Her coiffure and make-up, so artfully applied, were in excellent taste. What impressed me more than anything else was the straightforward, almost piercing expression of her genuinely beautiful eyes, blue-lavender in color.

This particular morning the Duchess's dress was a simple yet extremely smart two-piece model which perfectly suited her neat figure. It was light blue linen and the narrow patent leather belt encircling her small waist was yellow. The Duchess's favorite color-tones were blue and yellow. The beautifully cut brown and white spectator shoes she wore added jauntiness to her appearance. The well-chosen jewels – sparkling sapphires, diamonds and topaz in combination (and the lovely jeweled flamingo which adorned her dress) – contributed to the glamour of her ensemble and enhanced her attractiveness and magnetism. She extended her hand and gave me a firm handshake. I curtsied as was expected. She welcomed me to Government House in a friendly and cordial manner and then went over my manifold duties with me.

Like the Duke, she spoke with authority. Her accent was a cross between Southern and British. The Duchess told me I was to have a car and chauffeur at my disposal and that I was free to entertain at Government House any of my personal friends from America who might be vacationing in Nassau if she and the Duke were away, so long as I cleared it in advance. She was keen that I should feel at home here and presumably worried that I might be homesick for New York. From this first meeting, I admired the Duchess of Windsor and genuinely liked her.

This was only the start of my adventure in Nassau, an adventure that would last for four years. These were wondrous years, crammed full of hard, yet fascinating work. Contrary to the opinion of some ill-informed biographers and journalists, the Windsors were conscientious and dedicated. I was saddened later on to read so many ill-informed accounts of them.

Government House, as viewed from George Street, and a side view with Governor's Colonial Office within first level of the building to the left in both photos.
Source: Author's collection

MY DUTIES

Whenever I had started a new job in the past, I always got started immediately. Even with that approach, however, I was amazed how quickly I was absorbed into my new job at Government House, tackling a great variety of responsibilities, many with complicated ramifications. There is nothing like being busy, and I relished the scope and pace of it all.

My working life was divided into times reserved for the Duchess, others reserved for HRH, and then double deals for Team WE (for Wallis and Edward), their way of referring to their joint endeavors. Not only was I the Duchess's social secretary working in close conjunction with Major Phillips, but I was also the Duke's private secretary handling his personal and confidential correspondence. This did not go through his regular governmental staff secretary. I also served as his financial secretary, handling his private funds.

When we were in residence at Government House, my daily duties for the Duchess followed a fixed routine. As soon as she telephoned on the house telephone, invariably at 9.30 (but a little later if the masseuse had an appointment), I would present myself at her suite. The Duke and Duchess would be enjoying their morning cups of tea. Breakfast was informal and it was not unusual to find the Duke in his dressing gown and slippers, seated in the Wallis-blue satin-covered lounge chair, munching away on his toast and marmalade with the royal dogs looking longingly at every bite. The Duchess, a pretty picture in her chiffon and lace jacket, would be sitting up in bed sipping her tea. I would be on the sidelines, pencil poised for quick notes, either for something personal or some weighty government matter. Once the Duchess asked me to order a breakfast tray as a gift to a departing guest who had admired one sent up to her room.

The Duchess was methodical and consulted a list of penciled notes she made the night before. I then received the orders for the day to be relayed to the various members of staff. Later, in turn, the two chauffeurs would check with me for their schedules. In preparing her correspondence, I had to be most precise with my spelling. The Duchess insisted that some words be spelt the French way, for example "cheque" for a financial check. Some had to be spelled the English way – such as "favour" and "honour". Some I just spelt the good old American way.

The scope of dictation was tremendously varied and half the correspondence I handled myself. Perhaps the Duchess would be preparing a speech as President of the Nassau Garden Club or the British Red Cross. She used to worry a lot about those speeches at first – not their composition but their delivery. They were always well written (the Duke would proofread them) and thus easy to deliver well. Making speeches was a new experience for the Duchess and she had to find her confidence.

From time to time babies were born to members of the colored staff at Government House. The Duchess would send me off to choose a complete layette down at a Bay Street infants' shop in the suitable color when the "arrival" appeared. Then I would present the gift to the proud parent in the Duchess's name and with her personal best wishes. I was amused at the selection of baby names. One of the sons of Laura, the Bahamian cook, was named "Autry" after the famous American singing cowboy. There was more than one Winston Spencer Churchill on the roll of the Duchess's baby clinic, and after America's entry into the war, several Franklin Delano Roosevelts were promptly registered.

If there was a crisis amongst the staff, I had to appeal to the Duchess to act as an arbitrator. She was always fair. With such an international staff (Bahamian, English, French, Scottish and American) there were bound to be differences of opinion and clashes of temperament. Major Phillips settled most of them and I worked on a few. For example, a major discussion arose between the British housekeeper and the French maid over the minor detail of the correct way to turn down the sheet on a guest's bed – the French way as against the English style. Sometimes the Duchess would laugh if a query came up about the staff and say to the Major, "You just ask Miss Drewes. She knows what is going on in Government House."

One morning I told the Duchess that a forthcoming dinner-bridge party invitation had me worried. I prided myself on my knowledge of contract bridge but was quite out of practice and rather hesitant about being a fourth in this particular game where the other players were experts by reputation. The Duchess knew the threesome well for they were good friends. The host was the Bahamian manager of Pan American Airways, his partner an attractive American evacuee from London and my partner a wealthy retired Chicago socialite who lived in Nassau. The Duchess took me through all the points of the various systems of contract bidding. So I went into the game with confidence, though still nervous. I was not too lucky a fourth.

Most days, if the Duchess was not expected at the Red Cross Centre or the United Services Canteen for an early meeting, she would come into my suite and we would work together on some business project until luncheon. The matter at hand might deal with a Red Cross report or the ordering of a dozen hams, six crates of eggs and twenty pounds of bacon from the Lend-Lease army post in Florida to feed the ever-hungry service men down at the Canteen. Or, we might make a list to send to New York for medical necessities

10

for the Infant Welfare Centers which the Duchess had had constructed on New Providence Island or for some impoverished Out Island settlement. A few times, we formulated the travel requirements and tickets for a proposed rail trip in America, with the necessary hotel accommodations along the way and at the end of the line for the royal party.

I was usually free from one o'clock until teatime. I usually drove down in my Crosley car to the exclusive Emerald Beach Club. Here I was allowed to use the Duke and Duchess's former cabaña after they had acquired a more private one further along the west coast. There I could read quietly, write and enjoy a marvelous swim. Many a sock I knitted for the British Red Cross. They were blue so I assume they were destined for the Royal Navy. I used to write my name on a slip of paper and insert it in the toe of a completed number. I never got a response from any naval recipient so perhaps my knitting effort was not so expert. Then, back I would drive to Government House around five o'clock in time to take dictation from HRH. This lasted until the valet announced the arrival of the local barber.

HRH was conscientious. If he was in the midst of composing a report which needed numerous drafts and re-working (though he needed no ghost writer), he would bow out of a dinner party at Government House around ten-thirty o'clock and go into session with me in his private study upstairs. I would fairly pinch myself and say: "Fancy, Jean, here you are taking dictation from the one-time King of England ... in this fashion!" There the Duke would be, striding back and forth in his kilt, in shirt sleeves (for he would have removed his tartan jacket for comfort), puffing away on his cigar at intervals and concentrating one hundred percent on the problem on his mind.

He was always appreciative of my services and seemed relieved to be able to get his thoughts down in shorthand before returning below to join the guests, by then invariably playing contract bridge. If the dictation was urgent, my completed work would be on his desk for signature by nine o'clock the next morning, ready for him to sign. I would then seal the envelope and melt wax on the back for him to seal with his crest.

Sometimes the butler would hear me hard at work around midnight, from the patio below my suite, tapping out the Duke's words on my typewriter. I would respond to a gentle knock at my door and there would be George Marshall, the English butler, an impressive, stately figure standing six feet, three inches (a former Grenadier and Welsh Guardsman during World War I), offering a glass of champagne and a couple of English biscuits on a silver tray.

I found that I was not only expected to be a hard-working secretary in the mornings, during the tea time period and "on call" some evenings, but I was included in certain social appointments at Government House, which more than compensated for the rigorous daily routine. Holidays provided an entirely different working routine and social life, which I thoroughly enjoyed.

Author's suite, Government House. Note the drawing of Tilly the Toiler on the wall.
Source: Author's collection, photo circa 1940

Usually free from one o'clock until "teatime" on work days, the author frequently relaxed at her cabana at Cable Beach. She obviously liked her job, but kept her work shoes on in this photo just in case she needed to hop into her little Crosley car for a quick return to Government House.

*View down George Street to Bay Street from author's suite,
Government House. Christ Church Cathedral is at right. Paradise
Island (then Hog Island) is in the background across the bay, and
part of the British Colonial Hotel is in the distance to the left.*
Source: Author's collection, photo circa 1940

LIFE AT GOVERNMENT HOUSE

O n royal anniversaries or at seasons like Christmas, Marguerite, the Duchess's French
maid, tied wide, red satin bows around the necks of the little Cairn Terriers which
the Duke called "The Gangsters". This caused incessant barking as the dogs raced down
the hall in their trimmings, which they much disliked. The household knew the dogs
were en route to yap "Merry Christmas" to their royal master and mistress. The Duke,
busy making his own special blend of tea, would silence them with a loud "QUIET" and
proceed to interest them in their special assortment of canine toys.

Of these dogs, Pooky assumed priority. Preezie really had seniority rights and Detto,
the want-to-be-left-alone type, did not care much about anything, except when and what
he was fed.

Next on the holiday agenda was the distribution of gifts to the members of the Government House staff and the gubernatorial office staff by the Duke and Duchess. Previously,
the Duchess had personally wrapped all the gifts and attached an individual greeting
card bearing both their signatures. The Christmas list was a matter of importance to the
Duchess and she chose each present carefully. No one was forgotten.

One year, before America's entry into the war, I flew over to Miami in early December
and arranged for a grouping of alternate selections at one of the large fashionable shops.
Then, after the arrival of the Duke and Duchess in Florida before the holidays, the Duchess, the personal shopper and I went into session, visiting various chosen shops. The
gifts were chosen with humor. I remember a massive rhinestone lovebird brooch given to
Laura, who for all her 250 pounds and five or six offspring, was a popular romantic figure.

On Christmas morning in the library, Major Phillips called out each name in turn.
The Duke then made the presentation and the Duchess joined him in shaking hands with
the person and extending Christmas greetings and best wishes for the New Year. I was
thrilled with a Christmas gift to me – a beautiful gold wristwatch from Cartier's in New
York, with a facsimile of the royal coronet, engraved on the back "From WE Xmas 1941".
I found this on my pillow on Christmas Eve when I went to bed, together with a large
framed and autographed photograph of the Duchess in white evening gown seated beside
the standing figure of HRH in his white uniform as Admiral of the Fleet. Of tremendous
interest was the impressive riband of the Order of the Garter, worn across his uniform.
The Duke's hand grasps his sword. This photograph is a treasured possession and carries
a lot of memories because I had stood alongside the Palm Beach photographer as he posed

the royal couple in the drawing room of Government House.[2]

Next on the holiday program was the special Christmas service at the Anglican Cathedral. As was their custom, the Windsors attended divine service with Major Phillips, the two Aides-de-Camp and their wives. Since the Duke almost never carried any cash (his equerries always took care of the money), we had to make sure he had a reasonable contribution for the collection. This large Cathedral on George Street, suitably decorated for the holidays with an extensive display of royal Poinciana, was always filled to capacity at Christmas.

The presence of HRH the Governor and the Duchess of Windsor in the Governor's reserved pew (second row to the right, down from the altar – across t he aisle from the Island officials, the Chief Justice, the Colonial Secretary and others) added considerably to the occasion. After the dignified and moving service, the Windsors stayed awhile at the west door to talk to the Bahamian, English, Canadian and American residents and visitors.

On the way back to their residence, they called in at the Bahamas General Hospital to say a few cheery words to those hospitalized there. Flowers had been distributed previously among the sick from the Government House gardens, under the Duchess's instructions. The Windsors paid special attention to the little children in the sick wards.

Next, a small group of us was lucky to be invited to a light luncheon served on the outside lower veranda of Government House. This dining area bordered the grass terrace and the Duke's rockery, in which he took a great interest, even digging some of it himself. Beyond, the beautiful gardens stretched almost as far as the eye could see on either side of the palm-lined center pathway.

No holiday was complete without the joy brought by one particularly frequent houseguest, "Aunt Bessie". The Duchess's aunt, Mrs. J. Buchanan Merryman[3] of Washington, D.C., was a congenial and charming American lady. She was devoted to her niece and to the Duke, and was held in the highest esteem by both of them. She had a keen sense of humor and was always good company. I shall never forget first meeting Aunt Bessie. Among other gifts, she had brought the Duke a gadget to evoke a laugh, a toy mouse, so realistic that it brought a squeal from everyone. She was in the process of demonstrating it to the Duke when I chanced to come down the hall. We met amid squeals of laughter. I had the pleasure of dining alone with Aunt Bessie at the Duchess's request on many occasions at Government House when the Duke and Duchess were out at official dinners.

---

[2] 'WE' was also engraved on a beautiful sapphire and gold ring which the Duke and Duchess later gave to the author as a birthday gift.

[3] Bessie Merryman (1864-1964), sister of the Duchess's mother

Later, we attended the local cinema in the royal row, the first loge section of the balcony. Another time we attended the Adjournment of the House of Assembly. The pomp and ceremony of the occasion was much appreciated. I had a special interest in it for I had spent hours with the Governor taking down and revamping this particular speech, so it was special to hear it delivered.

The Duke and Duchess had acquired many close friends in Europe and America prior to their arrival in Nassau, and many of them came to stay at Government House. The guests included the Herman L. Rogerses,[4] who had been host and hostess to the Duchess at Cannes at the time of the Abdication and were very close friends, as were Sir Walter Monckton[5] and Robert R. Young[6] of Palm Beach. Baroness (Peggy) de Gripenberg[7] was a favorite guest of the Duchess. They had been friends since the Duchess's days as a budding socialite in London during the thirties when Peggy was the wife of the Finnish Minister. Herbert Pulitzer,[8] who later was commissioned with the Royal Air Force in Nassau, provided a close liaison between the royal couple and the R.A.F. His stepdaughter, Gracie Amory, was a very accomplished golfer and she showed the Duke a few expert pointers on the local course.

One of my favorites was Arthur Vining Davis[9] of New York and Nassau. Lord Beaverbrook[10] was also entertained on one occasion when visiting the Island. A frequent

---

[4] Herman Rogers (d. 1957), a successful Wall Street banker, and his wife, Katherine Bigelow (d. 1949), a young widow, befriended by the Duchess during her first marriage, when she lived in Coronado, California. The Duchess became a close friend of Katherine's when they were both living in China in 1925. She lived there in the Rogers' house for a year. Herman Rogers also became a devoted friend.

[5] Sir Walter Monckton (1891-1965), personal adviser to King Edward VIII during the Abdication crisis in 1936 and later. Later Minister of Defense during the Suez crisis of 1956.

[6] Robert R. Young (1897-1958), American financier, President of the New York Central Railroad, with homes in Palm Beach and Newport, Rhode Island. He provided a private Pullman train when the Windsors visited Miami in September 1941.

[7] Peggy de Gripenberg (d. 1979), wife of George de Gripenberg, died in Palm Beach.

[8] Herbert Pulitzer (1897-1957), son of Joseph Pulitzer, the newspaper magnate.

[9] Arthur Vining Davis (1867-1962), Chairman of the Board of the Aluminum Company of America (ALCOA) from 1928 to 1958. A noted American industrialist and philanthropist, he later invested in properties in Florida, the Bahamas and Cuba before the Cuban Revolution. He died in Miami aged 95, leaving an estate worth $400 million to his trust and charities.

[10] Lord Beaverbrook (formerly Max Aitken), (1879-1964), an Anglo-Canadian business tycoon, politician and writer, who owned many British newspapers including the *Daily Express*, the *Sunday Express* and the *Evening Standard*. Another close adviser to Edward VIII at the time of the Abdication. During World War II, British Prime Minister Winston Churchill appointed him Minister of Aircraft Production and later Minister of Supply. He accompanied Churchill to several wartime meetings with President Roosevelt and was the first senior British politician to meet

overnight guest was their delightful friend, Captain Alastair Mackintosh.[11] A World War One flying hero and long-time friend of the Duke's, he lived in New York but also had businesses in the Bahamas. Jovial and optimistic, he was the life of any party. There were also many other British, Canadian and American residents in Nassau who dined at Government House during the winter season.

The Christmas Day schedule continued with a large gathering which awaited royal attention over in the spacious ballroom above the Governor's office. Marshall, the butler, and his staff of four footmen – Gladstone, Johnson, Calvin and Sidney – plus two younger Bahamian assistants, had erected a huge Christmas tree. It was laden with lights and decorations. Underneath the boughs was spread a wide assortment of toys – trains, dolls, airplanes, dump trucks – all gaily wrapped in cellophane. What a din of childish chatter and laughter arose from the less-privileged Nassau youngsters!

The staff oversaw the distribution of the gifts and the serving of the ices, cakes and candy. Each child was given some sweets to take home for older uninvited brothers and sisters. The Duke and the Duchess played the role of real "Santa Claus" from the sidelines and it was a joy to witness their pleasure. Of course, this event occurred before America entered the world conflict, when there were plenty of supplies and toys and life was not on a completely restricted wartime basis.

As the day was a holiday with no formal duties, the Duke then set off to the golf course to improve his game. He played with the golf pro, under the watchful eye of the Scotland Yard guardian. Sometimes the Cairns accompanied him on his rounds, for which special permission had to be obtained since no dogs were allowed on the course. It was always amusing to see HRH literally folded in before the wheel of his tiny Crosley station wagon, while his six-foot three-inch escort and the three yapping dogs were squeezed into the narrow back seat. The Duke finally announced that it was "jolly crowded" in that sports wagon and so I inherited the miniature car which had previously been dubbed *The Jitter-Bug*. This car carried no license. Of course when Their Royal Highnesses traveled in their large, special black limousine, it sported a replica of the British crown. It had no number plate, and a small Union flag waved from a small pole on the front right fender. At other times this little flag was wrapped in a cellophane casing.

Meanwhile, the Duchess attended to household duties. After a talk in French with the

---

Soviet leader Joseph Stalin after Hitler's invasion of the Soviet Union. His book, *The Abdication of Edward VIII*, was published in 1966.

[11] Captain Alastair Mackintosh (b. 1889), a friend of the Prince of Wales and the Duke of York, married briefly to the film star, Constance Talmadge. Later a spare man in Palm Beach. Author of *No Alibi* (1961).

chef, Daniel Pinaudier, on the food details for that evening, and with Marshall as to the entertaining and service details, the Duchess joined the housekeeper and parlor maid to give a personal touch to all the flower arrangements which were such a feature in each room. The Duchess exercised extraordinary skill in blending colors and varieties of flowers and enjoyed the arduous task.

The Duke and Duchess did not agree about flowers. He loved them in their natural setting. The Duchess joked that the Island did not produce enough and sometimes begged some from the Duke's greenhouse. Most were flown in from Miami at least twice a week.

As a last household task, the Duchess personally supervised the table setting with its holiday floral decorations. The table held artistic Santa Claus creations, epergnes with sprays of red and white gladioli sprinkled with tuberoses and holly, and tropical fruit displays created by Marshall. The gold-rimmed china, the crystal and ruby glassware, the shining silverware and varied silver candlesticks holding the tall, slender, festive red candles, and the sheet linen and lace table cover and serviettes – all in their beauty – completed the Christmas atmosphere.

One after-the-party task I was amused to perform was to make sure that none of the expensive royal napkins with their royal cyphers had inadvertently disappeared, by accident or possibly taken as a souvenir. It was usually a male guest who proved the culprit. Sometimes I had to telephone the butler of a Bahamian resident early the next morning to ask tactfully for a check on the morning's laundry collection.

On the Duke's return to Government House from the Bahamas Country Club, his tea and biscuits were served to him by a footman on the upper veranda outside his suite. Here he relaxed for a few moments, rather than devote time to his personal dictation and accounts (the usual period of the day when I went into private session with him).

Next came the ritual of feeding the animals. A footman brought the dogs' food up to the porch on a large tray and HRH personally doled out their food from a larger center dish. The original Cairn terrier threesome expanded to a sextet while I was at Government House. Two likeable Tibetan Llaas terriers and a Jones terrier – Bundles, Yhaaki and Gremlin, respectively, joined the family.

Soon the valet announced to the Duke the arrival of the barber from town via the royal station wagon, and the French maid announced to the Duchess the arrival of the local beautician who would add the final touch to her evening coiffure. The Duke had his own barber shop rigged up in a small room adjoining his office which boasted a real barber's chair within and a striped barber pole without. I was always amused when on occasion, the Duchess would comment, "David, don't you think you need a haircut as

18

well as a shave this evening?"

The Christmas dinner was scheduled for 8:30. Guests had received their invitations, dispatched by Major Phillips and personally delivered by the royal chauffeur. There was a book at the small guardhouse at the West Gate entrance of Government House. Here various government officials, winter residents from Canada and America, and society evacuees from England and the continent could sign their names to indicate they were in Nassau.

The Major scanned "The Book" daily to ascertain who was in town and who was about to leave the Island on business or holiday. Furthermore, Pan American Airways submitted all passenger lists to the Governor's office as a war security check. The Duchess and the Major would decide on the guest lists for official Government House dinners, formal receptions and cocktail parties. A lot went on behind the scenes of the local society set-up. There were involvements and entanglements.

The Duke and Duchess were at the apex of the social structure and there was natural rivalry among the local hostesses to be dinner guests on the hill and in turn, to entertain them in their homes.

At approximately 8:25 (guests always arrived on time, never early!) I would hear the privately chauffeured and official R.A.F. and American Army cars arriving in succession beneath my windows in the left front corner suite, having been checked at the guard's gate. Then the uniformed police guards on duty would present arms as these guests alighted at the front entrance door. The Nassau policemen were a picturesque group with their white tropical helmets, their fitted white jackets, brass buttons and blue trousers bearing the outer red vertical stripe. These officers reflected the greatest pride in their posts.

Inside the entrance hall Marshall would be on hand, then the footmen and lastly the maid-on-duty, to greet the guests. Marshall was a commanding and dignified figure in his striped trousers and cut-a-way silver-buttoned dress coat. The footmen wore pinstriped trousers and short coats likewise with silver buttons bearing the royal coat of arms. Lastly, there would be the petite parlor maid smiling in her crisp silver gray costume with dainty lace apron and cap. All appeared pompous against a background of attractively-banked Poinciana and holly decorations.

The 26 guests would each be announced in turn by the butler as they entered the beautiful drawing room. This sumptuously appointed room was dominated by the Gerald Brockhurst portrait of the Duchess of Windsor[12] hanging over the mantel of the fireplace. I thought this a fine likeness, but used to think

_____

[12] Now in the National Portrait Gallery in London.

it would have profited from a minor touch-up around the subject's mouth to soften and perfect the facial expression.

At this point, having been given the once-over myself by the housekeeper and my little Nassauvian maid, I would draw on my long, white kid gloves and proceed down the upper hallway. I would peep over the banister, catching the butler's eye, to alert him that Their Royal Highnesses were ready to join their guests. I would then slip into the drawing room unannounced. In measured steps, Marshall would enter the room and in a most dignified voice announce, "His Royal Highness the Governor and the Duchess of Windsor".

One Christmas the Duchess wore a lovely gown created by Mainbocher – white crêpe with a Dubonnet motif stretching from her shoulder in zigzag fashion to below her trim waist. Just the tips of the Dubonnet satin slippers protruded from the hemline. Her long white suede gloves added height to her stature. Later, on removing her gloves, she revealed a stunning square-cut diamond ring coupled with a diamond-encrusted watch-bracelet on one wrist. The other wrist was adorned by a gorgeous diamond and ruby bracelet that matched the rather massive ruby and diamond necklace and her large impressive earrings of the same gems. Her dark hair so neatly and expertly coiffured, set off her striking features, and the jewels augmented the glamour she radiated. The Duchess of Windsor looked a veritable picture of grace – a lady of charm and refinement.

Standing at her side, HRH, fully decked out in his red plaid Scotch tartan, even to the silver knife in his plaid sock, was an unforgettable picture. The Duke looked remarkably fit and happy. How proud he was of his beautiful wife!

The guests in that drawing room reflected ultra-sophistication from the stunning gowns and sparkling jewels on the ladies to the resplendent uniforms of the various war services on the gentlemen. I drank in the smart and bubbling repartee all around me and soon found myself joining in.

Under the capable direction of Major Phillips, the most popular bachelor on the Island, the guests formed a semi-circular line. As the royal twosome moved down the curve, the Major in turn introduced the guests to their host and hostess. I was introduced along with the rest and made my American version of a British curtsy to the best of my ability. I was the only lady guest who curtsied to the Duchess. I always felt it a privilege to do so.

According to Court procedure, it was etiquette for the Governor's staff to greet the Duke with "Good Morning Your Royal Highness" when first meeting the Duke, and after that, to address him as "Sir" for the remainder of the day. I used to note how Major Phillips, who of course also resided at Government House, stood with head bowed on first greeting HRH in the morning. Rather than "Sir" I used to always address the Duke as "Your Royal

20

Highness" and I fancy I averaged that phrase about 100 times a day.

The next 20 minutes were devoted to a reception in the drawing room and the butler and his efficient staff of footmen served cocktails and hors d'oeuvres. A rhythm of sophisticated chatter continued to fill the air and the cocktails were not light by any means. They were real Nassauvian in content, mixed by the master-mixer, Marshall. I used to term them "potent dynamite." One was enough.

One jarring note was the snobbishness of the guests – that is, among themselves. They accepted me because I was part of the team and I did not experience any coldness towards me. Obviously, there was a rigid social scale depending on family, rank and cash amongst themselves.

On arrival at Government House, each gentleman guest was presented with a card informing him who his dinner partner was. At 9:00, the butler appeared at the doorway and announced, "Dinner is served!" On the hall console table was a chart showing the table's seating plan which was to be consulted before entering the drawing room. This was part of the Major's network of dinner arrangements.

The coupled guests passed through the gray and yellow-toned library on the other side of the spacious hall and then entered the dining room which looked truly festive in the red-candled light, supplemented by the crystal-bracketed, holly-trimmed side wall lights.

When so many guests were present, the Duke and Duchess usually sat on either side of the massive mahogany Chippendale table, in the center rather than at opposite ends (one place off from being exactly opposite each other) to allow a larger margin for conversation with their guests. The seating was arranged according to precedence and service rank. On my right was a Swedish baron and on my left, an American colonel – and what the Swedish gentleman did not understand in my conversation, the American did!

The Duke and Duchess were experienced conversationalists. They were well versed on practically all subjects. The Duchess was on several mailing lists for current fiction and non-fiction "best sellers" from America and helped keep her husband well informed on last minute world developments via the radio. They both spoke French fluently and gave the French pronunciation to many English words. The Duke spoke some Spanish and German but only once did I hear him lapse into the latter tongue, for naturally during the war that language was taboo.

On the banquet table, the individual menu cards were in French, for by request the Duke had the chef tabulate the dinner menu in his personal handwriting. The place cards reflected the English penmanship of Major Phillips. The courses came and went from the "Crème Vichysoise" to the "Bombe sans Danger et Gateaux". The champagne kept on

21

coming. No one should have been thirsty. It was a superb Christmas dinner. The Duke's French chef, Monsieur Pinaudier, merited the highest praise for his culinary masterpieces and the services of Marshall and his competent staff were equally excellent.

At the end of dinner at a given signal, when the port and sherry had been passed around, HRH arose, raised his glass and toasted, "TO THE KING!" Everyone rose and joined in the toast. The Duke and Duchess also always observed Thanksgiving Day with the required turkey in fitting American style. On this occasion, the guest list was predominantly American. The Duke's second toast on Thanksgiving Day was, "TO THE PRESIDENT!"

When the guests were again seated, this was the cue for the royal piper, who served as HRH's valet, Alastair Fletcher,[13] to approach from the upper terrace, swaying with the pipes in his inimitable fashion. Nearer and nearer he came until he entered the dining room through the French doors and proceeded to encircle the table twice. Then, he was off again, down the hall and up the circular stairway, up and down the upper hall, finally returning to his own room and putting his pipes to rest.

Fletcher was extremely proud of his musical accomplishment and in his kilt he seemed to take on at least two inches in height! Beforehand, the Duke always made a list of his requested numbers. He did so enjoy hearing the music of the bagpipes. At first, I did not much care for that type of music but I came to like it and then developed quite a longing to hear it. Fletcher used to practice on afternoons when the Duke and Duchess were absent from Government House.

Fletcher told me a tale that illustrates the Duke's sense of humor. The valet was Scottish and not over-friendly. His main interest was playing his bagpipes. He had served HRH loyally and efficiently in Europe and on occasion, he missed his homeland and pals. Disliking the Bahamas intensely, he sometimes forgot his concerns by imbibing a couple of quick ones of what the troops used to refer to as "cold tea."

Late one afternoon Fletcher discharged his duties of laying out his employer's dinner clothes – the kilt, the crêpe de chine blouse, the matching plaid socks, the black patent leather slippers with the shining silver buckles and so on – all in correct order with no missing items or duplicates. He was silently congratulating himself on his accomplishment inasmuch as he did not feel exactly steady. In and out of the royal suite he had weaved and circled, according to his usual routine, unconscious that the Duke was watching his perambulations with particular interest and a quizzical look on his face.

---

[13] Piper Alastair Fletcher, Scots Guards, had been the Duke's servant since his appointment as Major General in September 1939.

At this point, Fletcher thought it best to check on what he was supposed to play on the pipes that evening at the dinner party. So he made a sort of devil-may-care query, "Your Royal Highness, what do you wish in the way of tunes tonight?" The Duke gave the valet another all-embracing, up-and-down appraisal, put his pipe back into his mouth, thought another moment and then said slowly, "Fletcher, tonight, I would like to hear you play 'THE DRUNKEN PIPER!'"

The ladies then retired from the dining room, leaving the Duke and his gentlemen guests free to discuss world and Bahamian affairs. The ladies chatted of this and that in the drawing room and library. Later on this particular evening, as entertainment, a Royal Air Force flying officer played and sang a few of his own compositions. On other than holiday occasions, bridge usually followed dinner, with a continual assortment of tempting refreshments passed around by the butler and his assistants. The Duchess was a skilled contract player. The Duke very seldom joined any card game. After all, it would be a little embarrassing to pull a royal flush against royalty out of a common pack of cards. The Duke preferred to chat with other non-players.

A sign from Major Phillips brought the festive occasion to a close and the guests in turn bowed out of the scene. The last to leave, I shook hands and curtsied to my host and hostess, a chance to thank them and again extend my best wishes for the holiday season.

The final item on the Christmas Day agenda was the Duke's inevitable run with the dogs. How they enjoyed it in the cool of the evening, though I must admit, it was always a trifle noisy! A little later on, a few bars of melody on the harmonica would come drifting over from the upper balcony – HRH's musical contribution to the Nassauvian moonlight.

*A few of the Windsor's holiday gifts to the author,
1940-1944.*

THE DUKE AS GOVERNOR

As Governor of the Bahamas, the Duke of Windsor was popular, competent, forceful and well meaning. He was a wise and conscientious administrator of regular Colonial affairs and wartime activities. The Duke exercised strength in his decisions with a view to instituting worthwhile, long-range reforms and improvements. He strove wholeheartedly and industriously to do his very best in accomplishing his aims. However, his efforts were not given the support they deserved. The Bay Street Boys in Nassau, a group of white businessmen and landowners who exercised effective if not efficient commercial control of the Islands, were unwilling to see the Bahamas converted into a progressive British Colony under the guiding leadership of the Duke.

The Governor did a creditable job, but the Bahamas were not geared to advance. He had to battle the semi-tropical indifference and the natural resentment of the relatively few but powerful Islanders who held political power and were very rich men. They had no desire to accept progressive measures that would change the complexion of the existing set-up. As a result, the Duke had to deal with the serious consequences of their inaction such as a labor riot that resulted in deaths, many serious injuries and widespread property damage in Nassau.

To counteract his frustration, the Duke sometimes acted with impulsiveness to try to drive through reforms in which he believed. For example, as part of the war effort when the Islands were facing serious food shortages, the Governor created what was known as "The Windsor Farm" to encourage scientific crop raising in the Bahamas. Due to politics and indifference toward striving for a measure of food self-sufficiency, there was never wholehearted cooperation on the part of the government or the natives and the project referred to as "Windsor's Folly" did not enjoy tremendous success.[14] However, the Governor proved he had the potential faculties for doing an effective executive job, but this

---

[14] When America entered the Second World War the (Bahamas) tourist industry collapsed. The Colony faced possible starvation. The Duke appointed a committee to recast the economy along agricultural lines as it was felt that our people might have to subsist on a peasant economy and feed themselves as they had done during the First World War. The committee refused to take the responsibility of selecting a chairman and handed it back to him. In this situation, he showed a rare piece of wisdom. He resolved the dilemma by himself taking the chairmanship. Later events took a turn that gave the colony a new economy, and so agriculture was forgotten and the economic committee became a grab bag for politicians who wanted money spent in their districts (Sir Etienne Dupuch, Editor-Proprietor of *The Tribune* (of Nassau), *The Tribune Story*, London, 1967, p. 85).

post was not big enough to be worthy of his talents and the expenditure of his energy.[15]

I saw firsthand what the Duke had to encounter in the way of politicians in his government as I sometimes attended the evening sessions of the House of Assembly. I enjoyed the political debates (having majored in political science at college) and tried in vain to fathom the local arguments against reform. High in the realm of political oratory did I wander mentally with the local politicians – some very smart attorneys – and some of whom, I figured out, just liked to impress each other by hearing themselves talk.

On occasion HRH would reflect his annoyance in decided tones at being blocked by his Executive Council on some vital and progressive measure. But on the whole, in private life, he was pretty even tempered. One time following one of these frustrating governmental sessions, I was rather startled to hear his louder-than-usual voice leveled at someone on the terrace below. I walked over to the balustrade to see for myself who was the target for his sharp criticism. There stood a native kitchen boy with a very open mouth and startled expression. The lad was not too bright and I imagine his repeated inability to comprehend the Duke's one-syllable instructions about where to place a potted hibiscus on the terrace had worn out the Governor's patience.

The Duke was also the head of the Colonial Government. His opening and closing speeches to the Bahamian Legislature reflected very careful and painstaking analysis of the state of the Colony. Often, I worked with him on these comprehensive reports and likewise I was always interested to work with him on his detailed, confidential summaries to the Colonial Secretary in the Home Office in London.

His Royal Highness had an excellent command of the English language and was competent at dictation. He had a large vocabulary to draw on; he literally dotted the i's and crossed the t's for me. There was no doubt in his mind that he knew what he wanted to say and how to say it. When we were working together out on the open veranda, his dictation was often punctuated with hesitations due to the zooming of the Liberators in

---

[15] It was said before the Legislature opened or closed, anyone who asked for an interview was told that the Duke was not available because he was working on his speech. And he wrote a good speech, among the finest delivered from the throne by a Governor of the Colony. He also put a great deal of time and thought into preparing other major speeches because they were all of high quality. One particularly sticks in my mind. It was delivered at Clifford Park. I don't remember exactly what the occasion was, probably Commonwealth Youth Sunday. In a brief passage of this speech he clearly revealed a streak of bitterness against the Bolsheviks for the assassination of his cousin, Czar Nicholas of Russia, and his family. I cannot think that this sentiment could have arisen from love for a relative, for there was no love lost between the reigning houses of the world, but it was rather a feeling of resentment against a challenge to the institution of the monarchy (Dupuch, *op. cit.*, p. 84).

take-off from Oakes Field, not too far removed from Government House. I had many an anxious moment. As a perfectionist, the Governor drafted a great deal of his important, confidential dictation. His precise expressions reflected the nimbleness of his mind.

In personal correspondence to his friends, the Duke would write the "Dear whoever" in his own hand and also the valediction, before signing his name. I always had to gauge the adequate blank space for these insertions. In dictating anything with an international flavor, the Duke would ask my opinion as to the "American angle" as he termed it. He would glance over at me and casually watch for a change in my expression as to the shading of the particular angle. I was always reserved in his presence and never ventured an opinion unless he asked for it. His remark to an Aide-de-Camp came back to me – that he considered me "a nice, quiet girl ..." But he was aware that I had decided and forceful opinions on most subjects under discussion.

The Duke had a clear head for figures and far be it from me to correct his calculations. At the same time, two and two had to add up to four, as far as I was concerned. One morning I was standing in front of the desk in his study and he had the mathematical problem before him, all figured out to his entire satisfaction. For some reason, he glanced up at me and commented, "That is right, isn't it?" I hesitated, since I had my doubts. I answered, "Your Royal Highness, that may be the way you figure it, but it's not the way I do." There was a cold silence. The Duke was thrown off by this sudden frankness from his "quiet" secretary. He stuttered a bit and reddened. Then, after some quick corrective markings, he smiled a broad smile and said, "Hum ... now let's see... *you* win!"

It was officially the Governor who directed the war effort of the Colony. When I first arrived in the Bahamas in December 1940, many of the youths there were already enlistees for the Royal Air Force. I recall on the following New Year's Day I attended an afternoon reception at Government House. HMS *Renown* was anchored in the harbor and the Governor and the Duchess of Windsor entertained the officers. Present as guests were three of the Nassauvian R.A.F. officer recruits who were leaving that week for training in England. The Duke posed with each group before their departure.

Some of the local lads never returned to their Island homes. Later on, a number of the young ladies of the Bahamas, including two of the governmental stenographers and decoding clerks at Government House, joined the British Women's Forces and departed as volunteers for training in England.

I remember attending a solemn Palm Sunday Service celebrated at Christ Church Cathedral as a "National Day of Prayer by the Desire of His Majesty The King." His Royal Highness and the Duchess of Windsor attended the service in company with their entire staff.

After America's entry into the war, there was even closer liaison between the Governor and the United States Government. I recall clearly the Sunday morning of 7 December 1941. I happened to be listening to the radio in my suite and heard the startling announcement of the treacherous Japanese attack on Pearl Harbor. Immediately, I telephoned through to HRH at his private cabaña and told him the news. The Duke was obviously disturbed over the wire. I remember his prophetic words: "That is the start of serious business in the Pacific!" The radios at Government House and the cabaña were on and off repeatedly the remainder of that day and a series of private, coded cables were dispatched to London.

America's entry into the war brought the Bahamas into greater focus as a training place for the R.A.F. and as a vulnerable spot for enemy attack. A rumor went around that the Germans might attempt to kidnap the Duke and hold him as hostage. In my suite I had an antique piece of furniture, a remarkable affair. It was a huge mahogany structure with a full clothes closet on either end of a center section with three voluminous drawers and numerous shelves and cubbyholes. It extended practically the whole side of the bedroom. I remember telling the Duke that it was my hide-away in case of enemy action from above or long-range fire from an Axis submarine. That is where I would be found if I turned up missing!

When the war situation became more serious as far as the Bahamas were concerned, real enemy action did become evident in the Out Islands. Numerous ships were sunk and the surviving crews of these allied merchant ships were, under the capable and personal direction of the Duchess, lodged in a Bay Street hostelry. They were cared for and given adequate food and clothing by the British Red Cross Society.[16]

The Governor had an active supervisory interest in the maintenance of the Bahamas Volunteer Defense Corps which was trained and made ready for possible action in the area. However, as an added measure of protection, the British Government posted a company of Scottish Highlanders – The Cameron Highlanders – in Nassau. These Cameron Highlanders, a picturesque group in their kilts and glengarries (dress-up attire), later stood guard on the hill in place of the regular native policemen. Also, two Cameron chauffeurs

---

[16] The Duchess of Windsor was very active in war work here. She headed the Red Cross, which did a major job and the Imperial Order of the Daughters of the Empire which conducted a segregated canteen for troops here. She finally built the Infant Welfare Centre on Blue Hill Road with money from a private fund controlled by the Duke, all of which was very commendable except for segregation in the canteens (Dupuch, *op. cit.*, p. 90).

joined HRH's household staff in place of the Bahamian police officers.[17]

Very expansive and expensively-constructed airfields came into being – Windsor Field in honor of His Royal Highness The Governor and Oakes Field in honor of Sir Harry Oakes, Bart. The construction project was realized through the Lend-Lease arrangement under the supervision of the United States Army Corps of Engineers with an attendant American Medical and Special Police staff. Thus, in the Bahamas there were stationed British, Canadian, Australian, American as well as Bahamian forces.[18]

HRH was always a popular visitor at these R.A.F. fields. There was the Governor in the mess hall watching the food as it was being slung expertly at the individual plates in

---

[17] A *Tribune* reader who was near to the Duke when he was Governor, told me that he objected to an all-colored police force. He wanted to bring English policemen here to patrol certain residential areas of the Island. This is the practice in Bermuda. I certainly remember this proposal. *The Tribune* opposed the idea so strongly that it was dropped (Dupuch, *op. cit.*, p. 90).

[18] As the work of the War Materials Committee developed all kinds of people volunteered their services. People away from Britain were anxious to do something, anything, to help. One day a highly qualified Scottish water engineer offered me his services. I told him I couldn't use him in the War Materials work but that I was a member of the Economic Committee of which the Duke of Windsor was chairman, and that this committee was then discussing the water problem facing Nassau.

The sudden increase in our population brought about by the arrival of evacuees from England and troop and Air Force activities here had given the Island a water problem. The Economic Committee was entertaining an idea for building water catchments at Oakes Field. I asked the engineer whether he knew anything about the construction of water catchments. He said he had a great deal of experience in this work. I was pleased because this seemed to solve the first problem facing the committee--to find a qualified engineer for this work in wartime. I phoned the Aide-de-Camp and asked for an appointment with the Duke on a matter concerning the Economic Committee. He gave me an appointment for the following morning and so I told the engineer to see me the following afternoon.

I was so pleased with my find that when I saw the Duke, instead of going right to the point, I tried to play cute: 'I have just the man to build the water catchments for the Committee', I said beamingly. 'We can't have a colored man do this work', the Duke declared without waiting to hear anything further from me'. 'It is not a colored man', I said. 'Then we can't have a Bahamian white man', he declared, once again jumping to conclusions without stopping to think, 'no Bahamian white man would be qualified'. 'It is not a colored man, nor is it a Bahamian white man – it is a highly qualified Scotsman,' I said, laying the engineer's card on the table before me. 'Oh, that's different', he said, looking at the card.

But he must have seen the expression on my face that the matter was closed as far as I was concerned. I took up the card, bade him a good day without further comment, and left the office. When the engineer came to see me I told him I was sorry he could not help. The committee continued to discuss the water problem but never did anything about it. The Duke never asked me about the engineer and I didn't mention it to the committee. And thus an opportunity passed. (Dupuch, *op. cit.*, p. 88).

assembly line style. Although the Duke had already had his lunch, he said he wished to test it as it looked inviting. He did and then proceeded to sit down with his escorts and enjoyed a more substantial nibble. Since the food was Lend-Lease variety from the United States, it was good but servicemen are apt to be super critical. The reaction of the airmen was, "If HRH can eat it and like it, so can *we* jolly well eat it – and like it!"

As Chairman of the Bahamas Economic Commission, the Governor was interested in stabilizing the Colony's economic security. Through different channels, he tried to expand the fish and sisal exports to the United States and he was interested in transplanting the Civilian Conservation Corps idea from America into the Bahamian economic set-up. The Duke discussed all of these matters with the American authorities at various geographical points in the States. He arranged with the United States Government for the importation of Bahamian labor into Florida to supplement the critical shortage of American manpower over there, in connection with the planting and harvesting of the food crops.

He was right on his toes in the deal, and carried on the major part of the liaison work himself. He traveled back and forth from Washington making the detailed arrangements, and journeyed over to the Floridian camps repeatedly to make his own personal inspections in order to satisfy himself that his Bahamian subjects serving as farm laborers were cared for well. The job he did was commendable.

On one of these trips, we stayed at The Roney-Plaza at Miami Beach, which along with so many of the Miami Beach hotels had been taken over by the Federal war services and converted into an officers' training center. It was for men only, and life at the hotel was on a wartime schedule. Regardless, the royal party was lodged there for a couple of days amidst the complete Miami Beach blackout.

It so happened that the manager, Marcel Gotschi, was none other than my first top boss at The Westchester Biltmore Country Club in Rye, New York. We had a pleasant reunion. I was amused when I was driven up to the hotel. The taxi driver, a chronic conversationalist, told me that he had just had in his cab a distinguished visitor to Florida, the exuberant Mickey Rooney. In comparison, I commented that I must be a rather dull fare. Then, he mentioned sadly, "Say, you just missed Clark Gable – he was here – left a couple of days ago." I chuckled and told him that *that* was just too disappointing to withstand.

In the evening in the thick of the blackout, the French maid and I had difficulty in finding our respective rooms. We had to proceed slowly along the corridor and finger the set of numbers on each door to be quite certain we had the right number before attempting to place the key in the lock. It seemed that the war was being settled right on our floor. Far into the night there were "bull-sessions" of the officer-trainees – on the left of me – on the right of me – and across the hall. I kept hearing about bombsites and formations over the target et cetera. I was still as a mouse but I felt like tapping on the wall and shouting, "Quiet!" Probably the shock of hearing a female voice would have changed the strategy of winning the war.

When we checked out of the hotel to begin a very quick trip north to Washington and New York before returning to Nassau, the valet called my attention to the private checking that was being done on the sidewalk. The luggage was piled up with more to come, awaiting transport to the depot. The royal dogs were in readiness, yapping and commanding the attention of the curious bystanders. And there at a wide open vantage point was Walter Winchell,[19] with his secretary, taking a personal count.

OPENING of the Legislature by His Royal Highness The Governor, on Thursday, 20th November, 1941, at 11.00 a.m.

Admit to Council Chamber

Miss Drewes ⎯

WALTER K. MOORE,
President.

One of His Royal Highness The Governor's most important duties each year was to present his speech to the Legislature.
Source: Author's collection.

---

[19] Walter Winchell (1897-1972), American newspaper columnist.

NASSAU - BAHAMAS

That speech was prepared in the top left suite of Government House,
here closest to the Union Jack. The Governor's Colonial
Office was on the first floor of the building at the left.
Source: Author's collection.

LABOR RIOTS

I had heard tales of HRH's courage in the face of danger – how he had striven to be allowed to go to the front line in the First World War and how the British military staff endeavored to keep him, the heir to the throne, within a certain margin of safety. Certainly, during the labor disturbance in Nassau during the construction of the Royal Air Force fields, the Duke demonstrated his impulsiveness and utter disregard for possible personal harm to himself. I happened to be away from the Island on holiday so the following incident comes second-hand from his bodyguard.

Detective Sergeant Harry Holder of Scotland Yard had been assigned to the Duke's staff at about the time the Duke and Duchess escaped a Nazi kidnap plot in Lisbon just before sailing for Nassau. He held the Duke in the highest regard, and told me he had double respect for him after what he witnessed. He recounted to me how he drove with the Governor to the airfield where a tip from the police indicated that a group of the more violent labor agitators had congregated. With jacket flying, hatless and with a serious facial expression, the Duke with long, dominant steps, strode right up to the ringleader in the center of the agitation. Holder had his hand poised for lightning use of his automatic pistol and kept steady pace with the Duke but admitted he was extremely nervous at the possible outcome.

The Duke showed such courage and sincerity and commanded such respect from the crowd, virtually all native, that in his brave action, the tenseness and possibility of further violence melted from the scene. He broke the situation and averted another serious and destructive riot by asking the apparent leader and his supporters to discuss the crisis and their grievances later with a government committee and to settle the matter amicably.

A Commission of Inquiry was held, headed by an eminent English Judge, Sir Alison Russell. He conducted a thorough investigation of this labor riot and disturbance to the peace of the Island. The Duke was keenly interested in the findings which were rooted in the Bahamas' inadequate economic structure. Following his custom of keeping detailed records, each day I added the press clippings to the Duke's personal scrapbook on the inquiry, which could be used for reference by future Governors of the Bahamas.[20]

---

[20] Michael Hardcastle-Taylor writes the following summary based on several works listed in the select bibliography.

On May 28 1942, the Duke and Duchess arrived in Miami with several of their staff including the author aboard their own yacht *Gemini*. They traveled to Washington and were the guests of President Roosevelt at a small luncheon at the White House. On June 1, a labor riot broke out in Nassau, which at the time was home to about 20,000 residents, many of whom were quite poor.

The unrest began at a British-American Lend-Lease project just west of Nassau. This 'Project' was being constructed by American contractors at Oakes Field as the new home of Royal Air Force Operational Training Unit III. By treaty, local labor was paid at the prevailing local rate. The rate for unskilled labor had not been changed since the mid-30's and was inadequate. A strike was called at the Field and many of the laborers marched on Nassau. Confusion and surprise slowed official decision-making and police protection, and many of the businesses, shops and bars in the heart of town were smashed up and looted.

At the height of the disturbance, perhaps 2,000 workers had joined in the destruction and a general strike was called. The workers demanded government action to improve their wages and working conditions, well aware that American workers at the Field were receiving more money and better food for the same work. The situation was very serious, most businesses were closed and the white Bay Street Boys were beside themselves with fear and rage. Troops were called out led by a company of Cameron Highlanders, which had been sent to the Bahamas earlier to enhance wartime security.

Shots were fired and by nightfall, several Bahamians were dead and dozens injured. The businessmen demanded that the Acting Governor, Colonial Secretary Leslie Heape, restore order and derided the Police Commissioner, Colonel Erskine Lindop, for not acting quickly enough to suppress the riots in their early stages. A curfew was enforced and the Riot Act was read, literally and figuratively. Grant's Town, an all-black area, saw its fire and police stations burned. The Duke returned to Nassau immediately aboard a plane provided by the President, leaving the Duchess and the rest of his small staff behind in Washington.

The Daily Tribune in Nassau, wrote on June 13, 1942: "Today, when the balance has been restored, the feature which stands out above all others is the fact that it was eventually resolved into stability by the dominating personality of one man – His Royal Highness the Governor … His Royal Highness handled the delicate situation with tact and dignity, resolution and authority … "

34

Bahamian man and boy in Nassau. It was not an easy task for
Bahamian men and women to support their families in the 1940s.
Source: Author's collection.

Detective Sergeant Harry Holder visiting Severance, New York on 27 June 1944. The Duke and Duchess were well-protected during World War II by this man, their Scotland Yard bodyguard. Photo shows Sgt. Holder in his new uniform as Flying Officer, Royal Air Force.
Source: Author's collection.

THE DUCHESS'S CHARITIES
AND THE BAY STREET FIRE

The Duchess shared the limelight with her husband in the Bahamas, both officially and deservedly so. She is a remarkable woman. I knew her as a devoted wife and helpmate to His Royal Highness, an executive-organizer of widespread humanitarian and charitable activities, an author, a promoter, an interior decorator and a perfect hostess. I hold her in the highest regard.

Her activities on the Islands were varied. She took a leading and active part in the war effort and contributed unstintingly of her time, money and executive drive. Being the Governor's wife, she was automatically President of the Bahamas Branch of the British Red Cross. Under her guidance, the Red Cross accomplishments were greatly augmented and she devoted many hours to executive duty. The Duchess was an efficient worker herself, inspiring others to cooperate and give freely of time and effort. I might add that she looked so trim and neat in the Red Cross uniform she always wore on duty. She set a smart example.

The whole Red Cross effort nearly met with complete disaster due to an unforeseen event. Around 1:00 in the morning towards the end of June 1942, for some reason I suddenly awakened. I noticed an unusual reflection in my room, sat up in bed rather startled and my gaze scanned a flaming illumination of lower Bay Street. As my corner suite was located on the front left section of Government House, I enjoyed a commanding view of the harbor as well as the business district. The fire must have been sudden because all was quiet below. No alarm had been given by the guard on duty. His attention must have been elsewhere. I quickly reached for the house telephone and the sleepy voice of Major Phillips responded to my urgent ring. Immediately he rang through to HRH and before many moments had passed, the entire household was alerted to the danger, dressed and geared to help in the emergency. By that time, the blaze down on Bay Street was becoming serious, rapidly creeping up George Street toward the Red Cross Centre, Christ Church Cathedral and Government House on the hill.

The most worried man at the fire besides the Chief of the Bahamian Fire Department was Detective-Sergeant Holder, the Duke's bodyguard. As ever, he was on the scene to protect HRH. In this exciting situation, the Duke was in and out of the crowd like a flash, helping here and there along with the other fire-fighting volunteers. Holder found himself ducking in and out of the crowd after him, desperately trying to keep an eye on the Duke.

37

The Duchess took personal charge of the removal of all the Red Cross materials, knitted goods et cetera. The Government House staff helped load the equipment into the Duke's station wagon and other vehicles. Later, throughout the night, we sorted the mass out in the ballroom above the Governor's office. Everyone helped, with the French maid chattering excitedly and endlessly in her native tongue. Shortly after the last load was hauled away, the Red Cross Centre dissolved in flames.

Honors went to Marshall, the butler. I remember seeing him high up on the rafters of an ancient hotel on George Street, opposite the Centre's location and just below the cathedral. There he was testing the strength of the structure for contemplated dynamiting. In due course, this hotel burned to the ground as well. Next, Marshall moved to the top of the cathedral itself. This called for great daring on his part for he was not a young man by any means.

At this point I witnessed a dramatic sight. The large cross on the church was outlined against a frame of flames several yards back. Somehow that sight gave me the assurance that all was going to be well. And it was. The wind did not change its course and thus danger was somewhat averted. The systematic dynamiting saved the town which otherwise would have been a mass of charred ruins. We at Government House were all so thankful that the fire had been effectively and miraculously checked, for the mansion on the hill had seemed doomed.

The fire had begun in an infants' clothing shop on Bay Street. The owner, a local merchant, was arrested for arson. Fourteen buildings, some of which dated back 200 years, had been flattened by the blaze. The subsequent trial created a tremendous stir in the legal world of Nassau. I took time off to attend the sessions. The final outcome was the arsonist's conviction and he was sentenced to about 20 years in prison.

The Windsors supported many fund-raising events in aid of the Red Cross, funds being sent to support the needy in London and to other sections of the war theatre. The Duchess held a large Red Cross Fair in the gardens of Government House on 12 March 1941. She made all the arrangements with the staff for catering and supplied all the refreshments. American tourists (this was before the United States entered the war later that year) flocked in for the occasion and supported the cause admirably.

Members of the New York Athletic Club held their golfing tournament and convention in Nassau. They were lodged at the British Colonial Hotel owned by Sir Harry Oakes. I was especially excited as Russ Westover, the famous cartoonist and creator of *Tillie the Toiler* was one of the group. At the closing banquet, which I attended as a guest, Mr. Westover sketched an original *Tillie* in pencil and crayon for me and autographed it. *Tillie* hung over my desk at Government House until my final departure in 1944, inspiring me to keep working.

The Duke and Duchess attended two magnificent performances, one by Ruth Draper[21] and the other by the world-famous harpists, Carlos and Marjorie Call Salzedo.[22] Both times the charity supported The Duke of Gloucester's Fund for the British Red Cross and St. John's War Organization. These artists played to a full house in each case, and I was lucky to attend both.

The Windsors also gave their patronage to the various church bazaars in aid of the war effort, the Save the Children Fund and the Fighter Fund. They were always so ready to help in any way possible. Sally Rand's famed balloon bubble dance held at the Nassau Jungle Club attracted a huge crowd and the Red Cross Fund was well boosted.

Also to benefit the Red Cross, there was a world premiere of the film *Bahamas Passage* at the Savoy Theatre. This had been filmed in the Out Islands, starring Madeleine Carroll and Sterling Hayden,[23] both of whom were in the audience. The show ended, as was customary, with the singing of "God Save the King" and a color photo of the King was flashed onto the screen. Miss Carroll and Mr. Hayden were then presented. They stayed on in Nassau and I caught a glimpse of them cycling along the Island hand in hand, both very blond and bronzed from the tropical sun. It was no surprise that their romance blossomed in these idyllic conditions.

Then there was an evening auction at the Royal Victoria Hotel. This was a special event, precipitated by the actual washing up on the shore of one of the Out Islands of two survivors of a torpedoed vessel. Two lads from the British Merchant Marine service, Tapscott and Widdecomb by name, had survived the hardly-believable ordeal of 70 days in an open 15 foot boat!

Robert Ripley of "*Believe It or Not*" fame was on hand to introduce the two survivors to the world through the medium of his broadcast from Nassau. The Duke and Duchess attended the auction as did most of Nassau society. I went with Mr. and Mrs. J.E. Williamson of Nassau, formerly of Hollywood, California. Mr. Williamson, an acknowledged expert on undersea photography, operated the world's only under-water post office. Business was conducted in a huge cylindrical tank submerged in the harbor waters for observation of tropical fish and plant life.

---

[21] Ruth Draper (1884-1956), a noted American actress and performer of m
[22] Carlos Salzedo (1885-1961), French harpist & Marjorie Call Salzedo, /
[23] Madeleine Carroll (1906-1987), English born actress and Sterling Hay
American actor. They married in 1942.

Mr. Ripley conducted the broadcast very effectively and charming Lady Oakes was the highest bidder for the crude sailing vessel with its amazing history, her bid providing £300 for the Red Cross Fund. Mr. Williamson introduced me to Mr. Ripley and I surprised him by remarking rather coyly, "Yes, believe it or not, Mr. Ripley, I am a neighbor of yours. I come from *your* hometown – Mamaroneck!"

Another charitable affair took place on a beautiful tropical evening in Nassau. The stars twinkled brightly above the open-air dance floor and festoon-decorated gardens of The Silver Slipper, a Bahamian evening spot located over-the-hill and decidedly out-of-bounds to the international troops. There was an overall gayness in the air. The crowd, 98 percent native Bahamian, was in a particularly festive mood for it was 23 June, the Duke's birthday, and the Windsors were expected at the Grand Ball.

The Government House staff, which sponsored this fund-raising event in aid of the British Red Cross, was on hand to form the receiving line. The white delegation was composed of Marshall, the butler, and his French wife, M. Pinaudier, the chef and his wife, Alastair Fletcher, the valet, Evelyn Fyrth, the Duchess's maid, Marguerite Moulichon, her very French lingerie maid, Joan Thomson, the English housekeeper from the Shetland Isles and myself. The remainder of the group down the line included: Corporal Archer and Corporal Sawyer, the two Bahamian police officers, who acted as official chauffeurs, the footmen, the cooks, the parlor maids and the gardeners. They all shared the limelight that particular evening at the *Silver Slipper Ball*.

It was a very dressy occasion. For all native male attendants, the printed invitation instructed: "Full dress, Tuxedo or Shell Coat." The native ladies' evening gowns presented a kaleidoscope of gay, tropical colors and styles, some slightly exaggerated according to individual tastes, in floral print, checks, stripes and plaids. Some of the combinations were most fantastic.

It was 10:30 and the playing of "God Save the King" heralded the arrival of the royal couple accompanied by their immediate official party, which included Major Phillips, Captain and Mrs. Wood and Captain and Mrs. Drury with Detective-Sergeant Holder in watchful attendance as ever. There was the usual amount of suspense when the audience stood at attention and then a collective, "Ah! Here they are!" Greetings were duly exchanged and the royal party settled into the reserved section.

The evening was getting underway to Marshall's plan, when there was a sudden quite light, totally unexpected rain shower. The cement dancing area under the colored lights got soaked with puddles dotted here and there. But then the native band did their best to ise spirits by playing, "Don't let it rain, no more – no more!" Almost instantly, there was a cheer and everyone clapped, noticing that the Duke and Duchess had taken to the floor in the first dance of the evening.

They did not normally dance at public functions and had only meant to stay for 25 minutes. Yet there they were twirling around, in between the puddles and into most of them. The Duchess's exquisite white crêpe-de-chine Mainbocher evening gown swished the water and her gilded slippers were completely ruined. The Duke's patent leather shoes were soaked. But the crowd loved it and I watched from the sidelines. It was a spontaneous solo performance which rescued the evening for the British Red Cross Fund.

The Duchess of Windsor also took an active interest in underprivileged Bahamian infants. With finances from the Bahamas Assistance Fund (a trust established by the Duke when he was Prince of Wales) the Duchess had erected two modern and well-equipped baby clinics on the Island of New Providence. This work was organized in close coopera-tion with the medical staff of the Bahamas General Hospital.

The Duchess purchased a car for the use of the visiting welfare nurse. On clinic days she was usually present to interview urgent or needy cases and I saw the success of the work as I was a volunteer at the clinic one afternoon a week. Mrs. Wood (wife of the Duke's equerry, Captain George Wood, both of whom had escaped from Portugal with the Duke and Duchess and accompanied them to the Bahamas) also served there with me. She weighed the native babies and I entered the weights on their respective record cards. If the Duchess was not there, I alerted her to any critical needs.

There was terrific poverty among the natives on New Providence. Once I accompanied Nurse Alice Hill on her rounds and found the conditions to be appalling. One settlement consisting of about 15 shacks had only one huge iron pot set over an open fire in the outside center area, three tin plates and four tablespoons. It was a communal kitchen and everyone had to eat in turn.

I talked to an expectant mother who was standing by the door of her hut. She already had six children and was completely unconcerned about the coming event. In her shack the sole piece of furniture, if it could be termed such, was a dilapidated table. Some of the tiny tots toddling around the area had swollen stomachs, resulting from rickets and from eating too much dirt. Surprisingly enough, these natives standing casually around in the sunshine were a smiling, happy group, seemingly without a care or worry in the world. It was always astounding to me the way they sealed up their shacks at night. With such crowded conditions within and all the window spaces boarded up, how did they survive?

Considering the critical needs on New Providence itself, one can well imagine the tremendous needs on the scattered Out Islands which were only linked to Nassau by one radio in some cases, invariably owned by the resident native Island Commissioner. With the Duke's assistance, the Duchess single-handedly tackled the health problem on these outposts of the colony. I know firsthand of all this humanitarian work for I kept the records, contacted the various Island clergy and took charge of the distribution of supplies under the Duchess's direction. She kept in close touch with the Bishops of the various church denominations in Nassau to ascertain the needs of their widespread flocks.

Bishop Bernard, the elderly pastor of the St. Francis Xavier Catholic Church, was a kind and devout churchman. Through my liaison work with his islanders, he always seemed to have an interest in my personal welfare although I was not a member of his faith. When he heard I was about to leave on a trip to America with the Duke and Duchess, he always rang to give me a blessing over the telephone. I also worked closely with the newly-appointed Anglican Bishop, Rt. Rev. Spence Burton, S.S.J.E. He was the first American to be elected Lord Bishop of the Bahamas. His Enthronement Ceremony at the Christ Church Cathedral in 1942 was impressive. I had a vantage-point seat in the fourth pew.

In order to gain a personal understanding of the religious needs of the natives, I followed the advice of one of our footmen. An American friend who was visiting Nassau and I attended the annual convention of the Holy Rollers, about 1,000 of them. Never in my life had I witnessed such a show and I never dreamed such rolling would actually take place. We witnessed the twirling and excited gesticulations of the native rollers to the accompaniment of a regular jazz band on the platform from our seats high in the visitors' rear balcony. I must admit that evening I was a trifle nervous. Twenty minutes was all I could take after the rolling started.

Whenever the Duke made a regular inspection tour of a portion of the Out Islands, the Duchess took the opportunity to distribute the supplies to the island clergy in person, instead of sending them by post. There were hundreds of tins of milk for the infants and children, as well as cod liver oil and large quantities of netting for the sick and infirm as protection against mosquitoes and tropical insects.

In some instances, she supplied bicycles for the native district nurses, together with medical supplies and complete maternity kits. She arranged for these kits as a charitable donation from a large American medical firm (Johnson & Johnson) whose owner had a winter residence on New Providence. All this work was of necessity curtailed when America entered the war.

Drewes

No. **193**

Under the Distinguished Patronage
of
His Royal Highness the Governor
and the
Duchess of Windsor

RED CROSS FAIR

in aid of
The Bahamas Red Cross Branch
GOVERNMENT HOUSE GARDENS
(entrance west gate)
THURSDAY, MARCH 12th, from 3 to 6
Admission, including Tea, 4/-

The Duke and Duchess sponsored and attended many such events during WWII.
Two Bahamian charities benefitted from the Grand Ball cited below.
Source: Author's collection

Under the Distinguished Patronage of
His Royal Highness the Governor and the Duchess of Windsor
Sponsored by the Staff of Government House

Miss J. Drewes

The pleasure of your company is requested at a

Grand Ball

Silver Slipper Gardens

on Monday December 7th., commencing at 8 p.m.
Gentlemen 3s.   Ladies 2s.   Evening Dress

Entire Proceeds will be donated to
BAHAMAS RED CROSS and POOR CHILDREN'S FUND

Organising Committee— Messers. George Marshall, Jack Johnson,
Gladstone Wallace, Calvin Cleare, Audley Hulmes, Thomas
Knowles, Sydney Johnson and the Misses Maud Newchurch,
Erma Costford, Florence Symonette and Laura Young.

43

*View from Government House down George Street to Bay Street about
the time of the Bay Street Fire in 1942.*
Source: Author's collection.

44

The Duke, His Money, and Florida Travel

The Duke of Windsor was a perfectionist. He kept his personal accounts and typed his own sterling account records using two fingers. Due to the pressure of business and demands on his time, HRH fell behind on his accounting work and I was flattered when he suggested that I could help him (but only after I had served him for two years). He had worked out his own system of accounting and tabulation and explained it all to me.

In bringing matters up to date, however, the figures as I figured them were a few shillings out. At the Duke's request, I went to see the manager of the Canadian Bank and after quite a lengthy private session with him, I reported back to the Duke with the minor discrepancy rectified. The bank had made a slight error. It was truly a comparatively small item that could easily have been written off; but it was gratifying to see how pleased the Duke was to prove that his system worked.

Quite understandably, the Duke did not have financial worries. Nonetheless, he was mindful always of the state of his accounts. In due course after my arrival in Nassau to take up my new position, he was billed by *Your Secretary, Inc.* in New York for a full month's salary covering my services. I had paid the original agency which had referred me to Mrs. Roosevelt a nice fat fee. It seemed to me that everyone was paying. Anyway, the assessment was finally cleared but I shall never forget the look of appraisal HRH cast in my direction, as if to say, "You had better prove yourself worth it!"

Part of my duties involved always carrying a sizeable amount of cash for the Duke's incidental expenses and compiling an itemized statement to show him from time to time. Occasionally, the valet would give out money from his own pocket, and on our return to Nassau the Duke would reimburse him. Mears (who had by then replaced Fletcher as the Duke's valet) submitted a detailed list for my presentation to the Duke and I, in a magnanimous mood, made it an even shilling total, disregarding the few pence. The Duke double-checked my list and commented that I was out a few pence (not in his favor). I casually shrugged my shoulders in a gesture of, "Well, considering everything – the time and effort expended by Mears – that is all right, isn't it?" At which point the Duke quoted me the familiar axiom, "take care of the pence and the pounds will take care of themselves." The result was that the reimbursement cheque was made in the correct amount, down to the last pence.

Another time I came into the Duke's bedroom-study on some errand and there was

Mears practically taking the bamboo lounge apart. Facetiously, I asked, "What's up, Doc?" for we sometimes called him that. He smiled, though a trifle exasperated, and explained that the Duke had dropped a couple of shillings somewhere in the lounge and he had been told to find them.

The Duke kept a most interesting guest book in which each guest (overnight guests at each of the royal residences since his marriage) had signed, with the dates of their stay and in which house. HRH usually remembered to produce this book when guests departed, though sometimes I had to prompt the valet to remind him.

I recall many times in conversation and in speeches, HRH referred to his experiences in World War I. He hated war and the misery and separations it brought in its wake. On one of our trips to New York, the Duke asked me to do a little research work for him. Before the Second World War started, the Duke had made a sincere and stirring appeal for peace on the site of the Battlefield of Verdun.[24]

It was an appeal by him to ward off a repetition of World War I and another disaster. It was a fine speech, straight from the Duke's heart, and he was proud that it had been included in the *Congressional Record* at Washington, D.C. I remember tracking down that publication copy at the New York Public Library and having a set of photocopies made up for the Duke's personal records.

HRH kept a complete set of all his public speeches given in the Bahamas. Each year on Empire Day, he addressed a huge crowd assembled at Clifford Park. On New Year's Day, he would make a comprehensive speech over the local radio to his subjects in the Colony.

In April 1941, the Windsors made their first real business trip to Miami and Palm Beach. They had been to Miami the previous December to deal with a serious dental problem suffered by the Duchess and had sailed both ways aboard the *Southern Cross*, a huge and splendid private yacht owned by their friend, the Swedish industrialist Axel Wenner-Gren. This time the royal party included the Duke and Duchess, the Major, the French maid, the valet and me. We traveled over to Miami aboard the SS Berkshire and then drove north to Palm Beach in private Cadillac cars. The Duke had arranged to have a meeting and consultation there with Sir Edward Peacock, his long-time friend and financial advisor, who was then head of the British Purchasing Commission, and a director of the Bank of

---

[24] The speech was made to NBC in May 1939. In it he said that for two and a half years, he had kept out of public affairs and he proposed to go on doing so; he spoke for no one but himself, "as a soldier of the last war whose most earnest prayer is that such a cruel and destructive madness shall never again overtake mankind." No one wanted war, yet the world seemed to be drifting inexorably towards it. He appealed to all statesmen to, "act as good citizens of the world and not only as good Frenchmen, Italians, Germans, Americans or Britons."

England who happened to be visiting the United States.

In a loud voice, the Duke summoned me into the drawing room of our spacious suite at the exclusive Everglades Club to introduce me to Sir Edward as his "American financial secretary." I was flattered and enjoyed a few minutes' chat with the prominent British financier.

The Duke and Duchess created quite a stir wherever they appeared and always spread good will. We were fully surrounded by representatives of all the protective American services on this particular trip. Besides Detective-Sergeant Holder of Scotland Yard, there were: Captain Eddie Longo, popular Palm Beach Chief of Police, Gerald Hemelt, U.S. State Department Special Agent, Harry Tyson, U.S. Secret Service, Percy Wyley II, Federal Bureau of Investigation, and of course, the efficient and amiable Captain Eddie Melchen of the Miami Police Department. An unnamed private eye stood guard over the valuables within the hotel suite.

Nonetheless, we had quite a scare about the Duchess's jewels. The French maid thought she had placed a certain jewel case in one closet whereas, after a lot of excitement, we finally located it safely tucked away in another. I remember that the Duke gave me the sum of 500 dollars in small denominations as expense money for miscellaneous uses. I was so concerned over the safety of that roll that I slept with the money under my pillow, in spite of all the protection.

A very swank cocktail party and reception for 300 guests was given by the Hugh Dillmans, owners of the Everglades Club, in honor of the Windsors. Someone had told me their mansion was a two-million-dollar (plus) Palm Beach showplace and I checked the calculation personally. I was able to take the time off to attend the affair since HRH had requested me to meet a personal friend of his, Mr. Fred Bate, a radio official from New York and London, who was expected to arrive at Palm Beach airport about the time the reception was scheduled to start.

A chauffeur drove me down to the flying field and I met the gentleman and then proceeded to deposit him at the party. Having received an invitation myself, I enjoyed circulating and appraising the sculptures and fine paintings. The organ room impressed me especially. My duties were indeed varied, and I absorbed it all.

While in Palm Beach, the Duchess was persuaded by her friend, Alistair Mackintosh, to fly back to Nassau. It was her first flight, in a private, expertly-piloted plane owned by Harold Vanderbilt. The Duke was concerned over the real fear the Duchess experienced during that flight. She was obviously afraid and I felt sorry to observe her so upset. Her eyes were covered with a bandeau most of the time and her husband held her hand across the aisle. The Duke repeatedly assured her that it would soon be all over. The Duchess also had a natural fear of tropical thunder and lightning flashes when nature was on a rampage. Usually, she would closet herself in her suite. I remember on one occasion the Duke cancelled an important appointment just to stay by her side.

I was seated directly behind the Duchess during her first flight and was too tired from the hectic schedule in Palm Beach to know or care whether I was flying back or being rowed over to Nassau. I was well anchored with Detto comfortably nestled in my lap. My thoughts went back to the time I nearly signed up with the Women Flyers of America. It stemmed from an inspiring chat I had with the ill-fated Amelia Earhart, who was the guest speaker at the College Club of White Plains, New York. She was still in her flying togs, for she had arrived late at the local airfield. Miss Earhart was a charming, carefree, boyish figure. She proved to be a fluent and entertaining speaker.

It was a pleasant, uneventful flight and when the wheels of the plane's undercarriage finally touched the Bahamian runway of Oakes Field, it was like a tap on the shoulder. How happy I was to be back once again on the Island. The Union Jack was hoisted high over Government House on the tall, official flagpole, announcing to the Colony that, after a week's absence, His Royal Highness The Governor was back in residence. The large mansion on Mt. Fitzwilliam buzzed again with the usual excitement and activity.

The Duchess's first flight, Palm Beach to Nassau.
Source: Author's collection; photo by McClellan Photo Co., West Palm Beach, Florida, 13 May 1941

The Duke and Duchess with Sir Edward Peacock at the Everglades Club in Palm Beach. Postcard caption (on the reverse) states: "The Everglades Club Basin serves as harbor for yachts of the wealthy and the exclusive Everglades Club."
Source: Author's collection

THE LOVE OF ANIMALS

T he Duke and Duchess had a natural love of animals, especially dogs. I recall how distressed HRH was one morning when a newly-acquired terrier named Gremlin, a tiny puppy brought back with us from Florida, slipped his collar, slid through the railing of my veranda where the Duchess had temporarily placed him, and fell about ten feet onto the concrete patio below. The Duke's valet rushed down and brought Gremlin upstairs to the Duke, who had been hurriedly summoned from his office. HRH gently stroked the little dog that had completely knocked himself out. To save time, the Duke personally drove Gremlin to the veterinarian and was relieved when the diagnosis revealed that the forlorn-looking puppy would be peppier than ever in a day or so, and was none the worse from his fall through space.

Another time, a couple of sparrows picked the side pocket of one of the white wicker chairs on the open veranda of my suite to make a nest. Before I realized it, one morning I heard a few chirps from the new wee additions therein. The Duke in his inimitable fashion, manifested interest and curiosity in those little common sparrows. Twice on succeeding days, he stopped by to check on their well-being, notwithstanding the more elegant and far superior sets of lovebirds which fluttered about in attractively painted cages on the patio below.

The three Cairns were devoted to the royal couple. Little Preezie was the Duchess's shadow. Whenever she was away from Government House, he was a lost soul. He would wait patiently at the front entrance, hour after hour, for her return home. On the other hand, Detto liked to park himself under my desk at my feet. The noise of my tapping on the typewriter keys apparently lulled him into fantasyland where he could dream of food. He always managed to be right under the Duke's feet when mealtime rolled around.

Pookie was an opportunist. It did not matter whom he was with as long as there was some action about and the possibly the handout of a crumb or two – very much against royal orders!

Sometimes the Duke and Duchess would stay overnight aboard their yacht *Gemini*. I would guard the dogs while they were away. To help counter their loneliness, I would take them for a long walk down to the goldfish ponds at the far end of the garden. As soon as I turned back to Government House, Detto would walk alongside me and Pookie would run along ahead but then turn around and wait for me. But Preezie would scamper back to his mistress's door to await her return. He never lost the race.

The author at Government House with Windsor dogs
Pookie and Preezie, 1942.
Source: Author's collection

GROUNDING OF THE PRIVATE YACHT *RENÉ*

On one of several Out Island tours and inspections during the war, we boarded the private yacht *René*, which was on loan to the Duke from his friend Alfred P. Sloan, Chairman of General Motors. We headed for the lovely Island of Cat Cay. This sportsmen's resort paradise, operated as *The Cat Key Club* by a few wealthy American executives, was located a good distance in nautical miles from Nassau. Mr. Louis Wasey of New York was the Duke's host.

We occupied *Tismon*, an attractive pink-stuccoed residence on the Island. I lodged in the guest room to be on call by my royal employers. The rest of the party stayed at other cottages, abodes somewhat grander than the term implies. The Windsors enjoyed their visit. The Duchess absorbed the social life and the Duke enjoyed the deep-sea fishing. He also dedicated the new golf course named after him, *The Windsor Downs*.

I typed the Duke's correspondence on my portable, out on the terrace overlooking the sea. The expanse of tropical azure sea with the white clouds drifting by above was inspirational. In my free time during the few days we remained there, I enjoyed bicycling around the Island with the secretary to the Club's manager, who turned out to be a fellow alumna from Katharine Gibbs. There was a swimming area with its stiff-wired enclosure to make it shark proof. On one occasion, there was incessant barking from a small wire-haired terrier, rapidly pacing the shore back and forth, following the course of a large shark within the swimming enclosure. I skipped a swim after that observation, to be sure!

On the return trip, short stopovers were made at various tropical islands for distribution of the Duchess's supplies. We passed the spot on *San Salvador* where Christopher Columbus first stepped on the soil of the new world, named *Holy Savior*. An imposing cross stands upright on the shore in an impressive garden setting. We stopped at Whale Cay where Miss Betty Carstairs was experimenting with agricultural projects for the Out Islands. She was using fish as fertilizer to enrich the soil there in an effort to improve the variety of the diet for the natives living on the Cay who otherwise subsisted mostly on fish, peas and rice.

We also passed by the Island of Bimini, famous in Prohibition days for its gambling and rum-running activities. Some of the various island and cay names in the Bahamian group are quite quaint: *Andros, Acklins, Crooked, Fortune, Grand Bahama, Great Abaco, Little Abaco, Long Island, Mayaguana, Cat Cay, Rum Cay, Great Inagua, Eleuthera,*

Great Exuma, Great Ragged and *San Salvador* to name but a few.[25]

We were making good headway back to New Providence, expecting to arrive early in the morning. A quick, decisive knock on my cabin door at 4:30 a.m. brought me instantly to my feet. The steward told me in crisp tones to get dressed at once and report on deck and not to hesitate even long enough to pack a suitcase. I heard a grinding noise coming from the ship's motors and realized we were somehow and somewhere stuck. It was hard to think we were in danger, for the stars were twinkling through the portholes of my cabin and it was such a beautiful night. The Duke and Duchess were already on deck when I hustled up and joined them. HRH looked terribly worried and the Duchess was obviously nervous and upset. I had never seen her before with less concern about her appearance. She had a net over her hair and no make-up.

Although she looked frightened, her serious expression disappeared for a moment when she smiled at me. I was made up for the occasion. I figured if I was going to be shipwrecked, I might as well comb my locks and put on some lipstick. I soon found out from the Duke that we were lodged on a treacherous soft coral reef about 50 feet from the visible outline of the shore with the surf too violent for any possible landing attempt.

The ship's Captain looked ill with anxiety. He finally announced his decision that for safety's sake, the Duke and Duchess would have to take leave of his ship and board the motor launch. Very reluctantly, they obeyed the Captain's orders, for aboard ship there could be no argument. They were lowered onto the motor launch alongside *René*.

The maid and valet were instructed to remain temporarily on board; Sergeant Holder and I were to join the royal couple along with the Nassauvian pilot who was officially along on the inspection tour. A ship's officer and a crewmember operated the motor launch. Perched on top of the Duke's strong boxes, files and the Duchess's jewel cases, all quickly assembled, were the three little Cairn Terriers.

Dawn came and we were headed in a direction skirting the outer reef of an island. We had no idea which island it was for we were lost. The ship had gone off its course and we had missed the *Hole-in-the-Wall* light. I guess too many shipboard experts had jumbled the proper course. Anyway, there we were, all huddled in that comparatively small craft. We must have traveled 25 miles in this direction and saw not a sign of life on the shore. Finally and very luckily, from out of nowhere, we came upon an elderly native in a small

---

[25] The British Colony of The Bahamas in the 1940s consisted of 29 islands, 661 cays and almost 2,500 coral reefs, rocks and sand spits. Inhabited by about 60,000 people, the centre of government was located at Nassau on the Island of New Providence. With an area of just under 80 square miles, N.P. was home to over half of the total population of the colony during the war, most of whom lived in or not far from Nassau.

rowboat who gave us directions to reverse our course. We did so and passed *René* again, waving to those on board.

We were afloat in the launch for five-and-a-half hours and there was plenty of danger of the boat capsizing with such an overload and the heavy surf. There was also some worry about the limited petrol supply and some hungry sharks hovering beneath the surface. The outer reefs prevented us from proceeding directly to the island, which appeared uninhabited and completely barren.

Finally, the settlement of Cherokee Sound appeared near the eastern-most part of Great Abaco Island. How glad we all were to reach dry land. It soon became apparent that we had been skirting the Atlantic side of the reef of this big Island, which accounted for the high surf. We visited the Commissioner of the Island at his home, had a cup of tea and awaited word of the fate of the ship over radio. Several hours later, we cheered at the sight of *René* coursing her way into the harbor. Very fortunately, the rising tide had lifted the ship sufficiently to allow it to slip back off the reef under its own power. Our waiting-to-be-rescued hours came to a safe and thankful end.

Cat Cay, one of many islands visited by the Duke and Duchess during the War.
Source: Author's collection; photo circa 1941

CLINICS, HOSPITALS AND A CANTEEN

O ne of the Duchess of Windsor's greatest successes in the Bahamas was her United Services Canteen in Nassau, a place where the forces could spend their leisure hours. The canteen was located in the famous and fashionable Bahamian Club, owned by Mr. Frederick Sigrist, who lived partly in England and partly in the Bahamas. He was a British aviation magnate whose aviation design and construction skills had helped create the Hurricane Fighter, used by the R.A.F. to battle the Luftwaffe during the Battle of Britain. He was a close friend of the Windsors and just after their arrival in the Bahamas, he loaned them his house on Prospect Ridge during the renovation of Government House. He then loaned his Club as an armed forces canteen for the duration of the war.

The Duchess planned the arrangements for the canteen directly with the R.A.F. staff and spent many hours superintending the alterations and decorations. The cost involved was covered primarily by a large donation from the British peer, Lord Nuffield, supplemented by gifts from the Windsors themselves, Sir Harry and Lady Oakes, the Herman Rogerses, Mr. Arthur V. Davis, and Mrs. James Bush, as well as other Island residents and visitors.

Renovation work was carried out by skilled American employees of the Pleasantville Constructors. They helped build the Lend-Lease airfields on New Providence, and volunteered their services in their off-duty hours. The canteen operated efficiently under the guidance of Miss Bessie Amoury of Nassau. It was open to the non-commissioned officers and men of all the forces stationed on the Island. American and R.A.F. Officers' Clubs were separate entities located elsewhere.

There was another active canteen already established in the center of town, down on Bay Street, operated by the Daughters of the Empire. The Duchess, although interested in its operation, was not actively associated with that project. Many of the Island ladies volunteered their services at all the canteens.

The Grand Opening of the United Services Canteen took place on Christmas Eve, 1942. Invitations sent out read: "The Duchess of Windsor and Members of The House Committee, At Home, Christmas Eve, Friday, December 24, 1942, 5:00 -7:30, United Services Canteen, Nassau." It was a gratifying sight to see how the airmen and soldiers located so far away from home and their loved ones enjoyed and appreciated the hospitality extended to them. HRH and the Duchess personally distributed a supply of individual gifts from under the huge Christmas tree. The Major and I served as their assistants. They left before refreshments were served. I stayed on and did a little circulating.

The Duchess had urged me as a friendly American and rather a good hand shaker to help keep things rolling. On this particular Christmas Eve, I looked appreciatively at more than one snapshot of the "wife and kiddies" back home and listened to more than one tale of homesickness. After all, I too was miles away from home – but I was just too busy and enjoying myself too much to give lonesomeness a thought.

I remember an amusing compliment I received at the canteen one day in the line of duty. My friend, Mary Teagarden (a fellow alumna of Mount Holyoke) and I used to wait tables together. She had originally come down to Nassau to cover the arrival of the Windsors for her Albany newspaper and had stayed on in the Bahamas. Later, she became private secretary to the head Army Colonel (U.S. Army Corps of Engineers) in charge of the airfield projects.

Stationed out at the Army headquarters, she naturally had a speaking acquaintance with the Military Police sergeants who guarded the entrance and exits to the restricted property of the R.A.F. airfields. A good majority of them were from the Bronx and Brooklyn. Some of them were typical, amiable "G.I. Joes". Down at the canteen, Mary and I enjoyed chatting with them. We had a lot of laughs. One particular sergeant expressed himself as follows: "So you are both from Mount Holyoke! Can you imagine what I like about you two?" We asked in unison, "What?" "Well, you both walk like thoroughbreds!" Now I took that as a real compliment, although I never had been likened to a horse before in my life.

Mary and I tried to develop some sort of liaison between the R.A.F., the Australian flying crews, the real Londoners, the Scottish, English and Welsh airmen and the American MPs. They were an assorted, cosmopolitan group. This was all before I met my Royal Air Force fate – Brian William Hardcastle-Taylor and before Mary became the wife of Flying Officer Harry Holder, R.A.F., who had previously served as Scotland Yard attaché to the Duke as his bodyguard[26].

Major John Tolle, U.S. Army, a jovial and proud Texan, was in charge of the Lend-Lease supplies over at the American Army base in Miami. Supplies were furnished on request to the United Services Canteen in Nassau. John was the officer to whom I addressed all my request orders, under the instruction of the Duchess, for hams, eggs (thousands of them), bacon, cigarettes, tinned milk, potatoes, etc., – items needed so continuously and in such enormous quantity to keep the hungry servicemen not so hungry in their off-duty hours.

Many an egg was fried to order in that kitchen by the Red Cross volunteers who served as cooks in teams; and many a cup of tea was brewed, not to overlook the coffee

---

[26] In 1965 when this book was written, Holder was an Inspector at Scotland Yard, in London.

and the many glasses of Canadian beer and ale passed over the bar for a minimal fee. The Duchess endorsed a leading cigarette brand in the American press and thereby secured a huge donation from them for the men at her canteen.

A Thanksgiving Eve Dance was scheduled to be held at the exclusive Emerald Beach Club for the Americans in Nassau. As usual, I had been extremely busy and was not planning to take the time to attend the affair. This particular afternoon I was out in front of Government House on some errand when an American jeep with an officer seated next to the G.I. driver came through the west gate and drove up alongside of me. Quickly, I noted the officer's rank and the mammoth turkey on his lap, partly concealed in all its fancy wrappings. Then, I took a second, appraising look at the officer and exclaimed, "Why, you MUST be – Oh – Major Tolle!" Indeed it was, with a turkey as a Thanksgiving treat for the Duchess. With a little help, I got the turkey in to the chef who thanked him profusely and I attended the dance that evening with the gallant Texan. I remember waltzing past the Duke and Duchess and they smiled their pre-thanks for the Lend-Lease bird.

The Duchess also established a close liaison with the R.A.F. and American Hospital staffs. She investigated the needs of the hospitalized aviators and ground crews by repeated visits to the hospitals. There were a number of serious crashes at the airfields in training take offs and landing attempts on the fields as well as out over the waters of the Caribbean. The first one involved a plane ramming into a wooded section on the shore. Fortunately, there were no casualties. I drove out to see how it had lodged in the clump of trees and brush, having miraculously missed a native's hut. The crew had been able to climb out with assistance, suffering only minor injuries, but were in a high degree of nervous shock. As time passed, the graveyard at the Base told its own sad story. I attended the dedication of that Royal Air Force Cemetery by the Duke and Duchess and the Bishop of Nassau.

At the Duchess's suggestion, I visited patients at the R.A.F. Hospital and tried to cheer some of them up. I know I was not very successful with some of the patients who refused to talk and just gazed absently at me. The more seriously injured airmen awaited their return home to Britain for prolonged treatment and rest in their homeland.

Major John Tolle, Q.M.C. — Alianii !

CARD OF INVITATION AND ADMITTANCE

You are cordially invited to attend

A Supper Dance

given by Americans in Nassau for their

Armed Forces

on Saturday, March 6th, 1943

at Emerald Beach Club

Supper will be served at 8.30 p.m.

Bus transportation will
be available at
British Colonial Hotel
at 8.15 p.m.

*One of several Supper Dances for American Armed Forces personnel held at
the Emerald Beach Club. Below: Author's Bahamas Red Cross Society pin, Canteen
badge, her Expert Typist pin, and a Half Crown minted in 1932, four years before
her Nassau employer became HRH King Edward VIII.*

Source: Author's collection

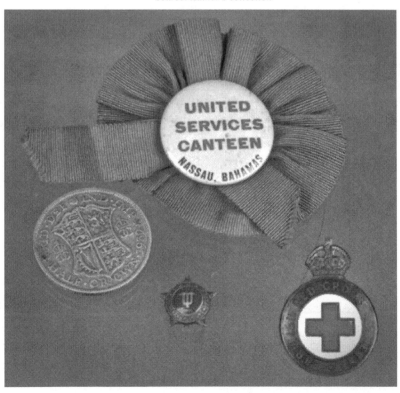

TRAVEL IN AMERICA AND CANADA

O n holiday, the Duke and Duchess devoted a great deal of interest to the war effort and building goodwill and liaison between England and America whenever and wherever they were called upon to contribute of their time and energy. I accompanied them on their trip to the United States and Canada, their first official wartime visit. This 46-day holiday began in late September 1941 and was quite a jaunt. The trip included visits to Miami, Washington, Baltimore and the Duke's large ranch in Canada. What a task it was to get the itinerary organized and to get packed en masse beforehand.

Packing the luggage for this lengthy trip reminds me of a slam article entitled, "The Duke and His Luggage," written a while back by a widely-read newspaper columnist. Granted, the Windsors never traveled light. Neither in my experience did the bag and trunk count ever reach the fantastic figure of 146 pieces, as suggested by the slammer. The newspaper coverage of the luggage seemed far to outweigh the more important war-effort news concerning the royal couple.

The royal entourage on this particular trip numbered seven people and the total of bags and trunks had to include consideration for the varied climatic extremes from tropical to quite chilly in Alberta, Canada. The length of the trip in terms of total time and distance traveled to the north effectively doubled our clothing requirements. Eight pieces including personal effects, typewriter, strong boxes and a stationary kit were chalked up to me. Also, a few empty cases were included to transport back Santa Claus's assortment of Christmas toys for the underprivileged children of Nassau.

We left Nassau by plane. Captain Robert Fatt, Chief Pilot of the Pan American Airways Eastern Division, was our expert at the controls. Captain Melchen was on hand at the airport to greet the Duke and the Duchess, together with quite a large assortment of Miami officials. The usual exciting reception and a short informal meeting with the press followed. We stayed overnight at The Miami-Colonial Hotel.

The next point of call was the British Embassy in Washington, D.C. We were met by a (reported) crowd of 10,000 people at Union Station. It was quite an event for me, an American, to be lodged at the Embassy. I enjoyed myself amidst all the formality but I was so worn out from the pressure of duties, responsibilities and travel details that I retired at 7:00 p.m. and slumbered 12 hours on this British territory. HRH kept various appointments with Washington officials, and made a speech at the National Press Club.

He also called on President Roosevelt in connection with the shortage of tourist ships available for the Bahamian trade and the Islands' pressing need for building supplies. As Britain's best salesman (as he was called when he was the Prince of Wales), the Governor usually secured hearty cooperation as a result of his enthusiastic sincerity. He liked to think of himself as a salesman for his beloved country. The Duke and Duchess gave a party at which many of the Duchess's old friends and relatives met the Duke for the first time.

Next, we were off via train on the long trip to Canada to visit the Duke's E.P. Ranch (for Edward Prince) near Calgary, Alberta. We stopped for a few hours en route at Chicago and St. Paul. At various points before and after crossing the border, the Duke and Duchess waved to large and enthusiastic crowds from the observation car platform and chatted with town officials who boarded the train at scheduled stops. They always appreciated the kind receptions afforded them and certainly spread a lot of wholesome British-American goodwill from that rear platform of their private car. I remember the Duke in boyish fashion enjoyed sitting in the engineer's box (by special permission) and adjusting the necessary controls, under supervision, to drive the train for a stretch.

On up through Canada we journeyed. At the depot in Calgary, a group of the Duke's long-time friends, including his attorney and his Ranch manager, greeted him and, in turn, were presented to his wife. In the background was a group of stalwart Royal Canadian Mounted Police officers, dressed so immaculately in their colorful scarlet jackets, standing guard over the royal couple. The Duke told the press how glad he was to return to the area.

One reporter asked the Duchess her shoe size. She answered politely that the size of her shoe could be of no conceivable interest to the public but she would be delighted to talk about the two baby clinics which she was establishing back in Nassau and the subjects of dietary instruction, childcare, elementary hygiene and pre-natal attention she was furthering.

We traveled on to the Ranch in a number of cars, about 75 miles from Calgary. The car in which I was riding nearly became stuck in about three feet of mud on one of the farm lanes. The Ranch itself, consisting of about 4,000 acres of land, was in the foothills of the Rockies. It was not run on a commercial scale, although the Duke took pride in raising some prize stock there.

The first evening, the Duchess invited me to dine with them and Major Phillips. The wild ducks presented by a friend to the royal party on a stopover of the train at a nearby junction proved a delicious treat. After dinner, we sat before the huge fireplace and chatted. I tried to look warm and comfortable but I certainly had the shivers, even in my long-sleeved dinner gown.

The Duke related an amusing anecdote about his previous visit to the Ranch some years before. It seemed that he was then traveling incognito under the name of "Lord Renfrew". His valet sent his dress shirts to the local laundry and when they returned, he noted with dismay that the inside of the collar bore the bold, black lettering, "LORD". HRH chuckled and commented jokingly, "I just told my valet before dinner that this time I am anticipating the return of my dress shirts marked "DOOK"!

The next morning the Major had a hearty laugh at my expense. We had been on an inspection tour of the Ranch and somehow or other I found myself in the bull enclosure. The Major was on the other side of the fence. Suddenly, I looked at the pensive creature not too far away from me and I guess the bull wanted a closer look. He started to paw the dirt and the space between us began to narrow. Luckily, I pulled a faster one on the bull than the bull had an opportunity to pull on me. Just in time, I ducked under the fence.

HRH visited two nearby airfields which were an integral part of the Commonwealth's tremendous program of air training. He noted the enrollment of many Americans as he had of Canadian and British subjects in the training centers in Florida a few weeks before. The Duchess made a tour of the Red Cross centers and kindred fund-raising units scattered about the area.

I remained at the Ranch for three days and then was off on a well-earned week's holiday to visit my family in California. I traveled through the awe-inspiring Canadian Rockies by train to Vancouver, and then flew down to Seattle, Portland and then to Oakland.

A fellow passenger on the plane was HRH Archduke Otto of Austria. During the stopover at Portland, the Archduke and his equerry remained in the plane to avoid press attention. I started out to catch a breath of fresh air but decided to catch it at the doorway of the plane. We were of a kindred mind regarding joining the crowd outside. According to the reporters' version, the Archduke and I, both incognito, had discussed the affairs of the world and possible solutions for impending crises. Actually, we were too exhausted to bother much about each other's state of health, wealth or slant on world events.

After my brief vacation on the west coast, I flew back to Chicago and rejoined the Duke and Duchess and two Special Agents of the State Department, Messrs. Basserman and Hemelt. They were accompanying the royal couple as a special escort, and had bid us farewell when we had crossed the border into Canada. They rejoined the entourage when it re-entered the United States.

Next on the itinerary was Baltimore, the Duchess's hometown, where the couple was given a great welcome by a very large crowd. The Duke and Duchess stayed at Salona Farms, the country estate of General Henry M. Warfield (her uncle) in Timonium, Maryland. The spacious homestead was set in the beautiful Maryland countryside among the dogwood trees, not too far from Oldfields School which the Duchess had attended many years before. I remember a huge flock of wild turkeys cruising over the lawn in the sloped distance at the farm.

The press was much in attendance and the Windsors posed for innumerable pictures. Mr. Alfred Sloan, Chairman of General Motors, called to welcome the couple to Baltimore. The Duchess's family impressed me. General and Mrs. Warfield were kind to me, as were the Duchess's cousin and her husband, Mr. and Mrs. Z.R. Lewis. I was invited to join the afternoon tea party.

As space was completely allocated at the farmhouse, I stayed at the Belvedere Hotel in Baltimore and a chauffeur taxied me back and forth for duty each day. I had a lot of business and social appointments to arrange, various appointments with special fitters from Mainbocher and the hair stylist, Roger Vergnes, both from New York. The Duchess's attention to her hair reminded me of the time I had my hair excellently shampooed in Paris, somewhere along the Rue de la Paix during a college trip. The shampoo was all done with the aid of a pint of kerosene and a sponge! The beautician, an artistic-looking Frenchman, was quite insulted when I queried him in broken French as to when he was going to apply the soap and water. However, I never had a better shampoo.

A large reception was given by the Mayor of Baltimore at the Baltimore Country Club in honor of the Duke and Duchess of Windsor. I was a stranger in this particular city, but armed with an engraved invitation and a friendly smile, I attended the affair along with many other spectators. I enjoyed watching the Duchess on the receiving line proudly introducing her royal husband to all her hometown friends. The couple also enjoyed a motorcade through the city and the cheers of about 200,000 people.

Leaving Baltimore and all the attendant fanfare and excitement, we moved to the Waldorf Towers on Park Avenue, New York. I was extremely impressed with my own accommodations on that first visit. Since there was no small suite available on the same floor with my employers, I occupied what there was – a drawing room converted into an office, two bedrooms, a kitchenette and bathroom. Naturally, some of my close friends dropped in to see me at the Waldorf when I was off-duty and told me I was doing extremely well for myself. During the daily schedule, one bedroom was used as an additional office – a sort of package and flower-receiving room.

Besides Miss Kay Nelson, I had two other secretarial assistants from the New York office of The Nassau Development Board to help cope with the telephone calls and mail which flooded in for attention. Acknowledging flowers and gifts sent to the Duchess by friends alone required the services of one outside secretary. Miss Nelson occupied herself with the Duchess's personal requirements and I concentrated on HRH's multitudinous needs.

At The Towers the royal party was well protected. Some evenings I used to enjoy relaxing by chatting with the police and press reporters on special duty. I was in a position to check up on all the latest front-page scoops. There were elaborate protective arrangements on this first visit and a motorcycle escort was always on call.

A press conference was held in the Starlight Room of the Waldorf-Astoria Hotel. The Windsors, amid a barrage of newspapermen and women, as well as newsreel and newspaper photographers, stood up well under the real strain. They were very friendly with reporters. Nonetheless, several extremely exaggerated and unkind reports later appeared in the press. Most of the unfair criticism was levelled at the Duchess.

An expert but very prejudiced lady columnist wrote an article entitled, "The Duchess of Windsor" which appeared in the "American Mercury" about this time. She wrote that "the Duchess never wears her jewels twice in succession ... The Duchess has often said she didn't think a woman in her position should wear a dress more than once! On this trip the Duchess bought 14 outfits from Mainbocher, 23 hats from Bergdorf-Goodman ... The Duchess's purchases average 100 dresses a year at an average cost of $250 apiece!"

Now, all that statement is nonsense. Naturally, to replenish her wartime wardrobe, the Duchess made a few selections, possibly a half-dozen gowns from Mainbocher and an equal number of dresses from Miss Hattie Carnegie. She also purchased about six chapeaux from Miss Jessica at Bergdorf-Goodman. I know, for I settled the accounts. These erroneous reports were upsetting to the Duchess who tried always to do the right thing, thereby avoiding any possible criticism.

On occasion I was interviewed by reporters who wished to ascertain my personal ideas on life and the rules to follow as a presumably successful secretary in a high war post. I told them that above all, it was important to be well-trained technically. Then, pick your boss! Choose the business in which you have a genuine interest. Work industriously and see any assignment through to a successful finish. Be close mouthed, loyal, dependable and resourceful. Be attentive to your personal appearance. Be enthusiastic over a variety of outside interests. Be cheerful and if not blessed with a sense of humor, develop one.

Crowded into their busy daily schedule were visits by the Windsors to the British War Relief and Red Cross Centres. Arrangements were made for the royal couple's inspection of the British-American Ambulance Corps, Bundles for Britain, Merchants Navy Club, Union Jack Club and the R.A.F. Benevolent Fund headquarters. HRH always enjoyed his visits to the Boys' Club and to the American Museum of Natural History in New York in company with Messrs. Cutting and Vernay, officials of the museum, who were his good friends (and winter residents of Nassau).

The Governor was in touch with his Colonial Government in the Bahamas. It was not unusual for me to be awakened in the middle of the night by a British-accented voice on the phone, informing me that an urgent, secret cable from British Intelligence in London had just arrived at the British Consulate in New York for the Governor and was in the process of being decoded for immediate delivery. I would then await its arrival at the hotel by special messenger.

Then, I would ring through to HRH's suite and within a few moments, would personally deliver the secret message to my employer, gowned in robe and slippers, looking very sleepy. I was under the Duke's explicit instructions to interrupt any daily conference or dinner engagement et cetera, at any time, in order to speak with him on a matter that I considered urgent and necessary. Sandwiched in between this full schedule, I had sessions with the Duke's American attorney down on Wall Street. I had my finger in everything, even to witnessing along with Major Phillips important royal and legal documents of a most personal nature.

A couple of incidents on this and subsequent visits to New York still bring a smile to my face. One morning after our arrival in town the night before, things were still unorganized. I had not had the opportunity to familiarize myself with the physical layout of the royal suite and suffered a major embarrassment, fortunately without witnesses. Summoned to the Duchess's dressing room to take a few notes, I got a trifle confused en route with the series of doors. After a quick, too-soft knock on one particular door, I barged into a room, notebook and pencil in hand. I nearly fainted on the spot for there was HRH peacefully asleep in bed. Never did I make a hastier or a quieter exit from any room.

On another visit, Their Royal Highnesses occupied a spacious suite very near the top floor of the hotel. I used to take dictation from the Duke in the drawing room, easily 50 feet in length and I would guess 30 feet or more in width. In between phrases, I would cast a look in the direction of the beautiful glass chandelier centered overhead. The swaying of that object – and oh did it sway – simply fascinated me. I would find myself swaying with it until I was brought back to reality by, "Will you kindly repeat that last sentence, Miss Drewes?"

Although HRH was reserved and serious with strangers, his warm human interest was always close to the surface. On one visit to New York, he was very concerned about an upcoming tooth extraction. I had made the dental arrangements with a specialist. The valet and I happened to see him off at the hotel elevator and informally wished him well. A while later on, quite buoyant and obviously relieved from the worry of the ordeal, the

Duke exclaimed to us on stepping out of the elevator upon his return to the hotel, "It's OUT and it really didn't hurt!" Furthermore, he expressed interest in the nice ride he had just had, solo in the taxicab, without protective escort. He commented that the driver had immediately recognized him and they had had such an interesting chat.

The Duke's E.P. Ranch (for Edward Prince) as it looked during his visit with the Duchess in October, 1941. Roughly 75 miles from Calgary, Alberta, it consisted of about 4,000 acres in the foothills of the Canadian Rockies. The Duke acquired the ranch in the midst of his world travels about 20 years before at the height of his fame as HRH The Prince of Wales, "Britain's Best Salesman".
Source: Author's collection

*The Duke and Duchess of Windsor with ranch hands at Duke's E.P. Ranch
near Calgary, Alberta, in 1941.*
Source: Author's collection

Author at the Duke of Windsor's E.P. Ranch, Calgary, Alberta.
Source: Author's collection

SOCIAL MERRY-GO-ROUND AT THE WALDORF TOWERS

S prinkled in between the heavy schedule of business and charitable appointments was a veritable social merry-go-round in the royal suite at the Waldorf Towers. Celebrities came and went and often I did not even rise from my desk to get a better glance at whomever the valet happened to be ushering down the corridor to meet His Royal Highness or the Duchess, or both. In some cases, I made the introduction myself. Former President Herbert Hoover was always friendly and gracious, a dignified figure. The Duke had the highest regard for him and whenever Mr. Hoover was in town, the two usually enjoyed a visit and discussed the affairs of the world. Lady Mendl (Elsie de Wolfe) came in to see me, introducing herself. At the time, she was very frail and petite. I enjoyed a chat with her about Paris.

Another time, the Duke called me into the drawing room and introduced me to his caller, actor Adolph Menjou, who had just returned from an extended tour of American military camps in Africa and was in the process of showing the Duke a huge stream of flyers' signatures on dollar bills, all attached together. He was casual in his manner and most cordial. Other interesting Hollywood personalities that visited were Fred Astaire and Douglas Fairbanks, Jr., both of whom were long-time friends of the Duke.

Juan Trippe, the founder of Pan American Airways, was a favorite visitor of the Duke's. They shared a strong mutual interest in aviation. Pan Am was based in Florida and enjoyed much of its early growth in Caribbean routes, having made its first flight from Key West to Havana in 1927. Mr. Trippe never missed an opportunity to call on the Duke and Duchess if their paths happened to cross in Miami or New York. Other popular visitors and more frequent guests were his close friends, perennial New York and Palm Beach bachelor Milton "Doc" Holden and Charles Cushing.

In and around the Waldorf, I was always brushing by motion picture or stage celebrities. I particularly recall the suave Raymond Massey, so distinguished looking. Ilka Chase and Irene Dunne were so attractive and exquisitely groomed, and I'll never forget Miss Greta Garbo's patrician features under a terrifically large brimmed hat, and her flat-heeled shoes.

Thanks to the thoughtfulness of Mr. Lucius Boomer,[27] head of the Waldorf-Astoria Hotel at that time, a very pleasant evening's entertainment was arranged for my enjoyment,

---

[27] Lucius M. Boomer, who bought the Waldorf-Astoria in 1918 and ran it with his Norwegian wife until his death in 1947.

all in the line of good business promotion. The invitation included me and a party of three, but only my brother Wallace and his wife accompanied me. Mr. Boomer always addressed me as "Colonel Drewes" with a smile in his eye, for I must have impressed him as an effective order-giver. As our association grew in succeeding visits to the Towers, my commission was raised to "General". When I chanced to meet him and his wife in the elevator one evening, I know Mrs. Boomer could not quite figure out my "title".

The particular evening I mentioned above, I received a lovely orchid by special messenger with a card enclosed, "Compliments of Mr. Boomer". When my sister-in-law and brother arrived in evening attire, I pondered a moment and came to a conclusion. If I wore an orchid, Dorothy should wear an orchid too. The Duke and Duchess had left the city for the weekend and the collection of six or seven choice orchids in their suite were doomed to wilt. So I borrowed one.

We taxied to Radio City, sat in the reserved seats at the Music Hall, saw the stage show from the wings and toured the dressing and practice rooms of the dancers. We then went into the projection room and noted the several showings of the same film running simultaneously to insure against any possible film breakage. We also signed the huge guest book right under the last signers from the previous night – signing as "Edward" and "Wallis Windsor." Then, we taxied back to the Waldorf and took our place at a table reserved for us in the Wedgwood Room.

Paul Draper gave a marvelous dancing performance and we met the famous jazz player, Eddie Duchin, who was entertaining at the piano. We had a midnight supper and toasted with champagne the Waldorf, Mr. Boomer and Mr. Frank Ready, Manager of the Towers, who had joined our party. As the last train on the New Haven line had long since left Grand Central Station, the Drewes family, a little weary but still fit, had to journey back to Mount Vernon via the subway, minus the orchid which I returned to the royal suite.

One incident afforded me the most amusement of anything that happened while I was residing at the Towers, and came as quite a surprise. A note delivered to me from another apartment occupant by Mr. Ready began, "You may have heard of me – I'm the movie actor, Ray Milland … " He went on to explain that his wife had an autograph book, sort of a family heirloom, which contained a remarkable collection of famous signatures, and he would be ever grateful if by some manner or means, I was able to secure the autographs of the Duke and Duchess of Windsor.

In glancing through the album which he had sent along with the note, I saw for myself that it was a tremendously valuable collection, containing such names as General John. J. Pershing, M. Clemenceau and President Woodrow Wilson (all from World War I). Now and then by special request the Duke and Duchess would sign an autograph album but more often they would choose not to do so. I had been impressed by the Milland collection, so I gave HRH a sales talk on adding his and the Duchess's signatures. I was successful.

The following morning, although I was rushed for we were leaving on the mid-day train for Miami, I had just enough curiosity to decide to deliver the album myself and meet the gentleman whom I had always admired on the movie screen. Down I went in the elevator with book in hand and rang the bell of Mr. Milland's apartment. I waited a moment and then another. No response. Then, I heard a loud voice approaching the door "I'm coming ... " The door opened and I opened my mouth and kept it open. For there, dripping wet, wrapped up in a huge bath towel, with bare feet and hair completely concealing his eyes, suffering a moment of nonchalant embarrassment, stood Ray Milland, his own handsome self. He laughed after he got a glimpse of me and I smiled when I found words to explain that I was the bellhop replacement. On taking the autograph album from my outstretched hand, he thanked me profusely. He then said he was sorry, but under the circumstances he could hardly ask me in – and I whisked myself away from the door.

Next, without hardly realizing it, we were packed and off for Miami – the complete royal entourage. Being in my usual state of exhaustion, I slept practically the whole train journey down to Florida. We checked in at the Miami Biltmore Hotel for a short stopover. The two top floors, which had been the private apartments of the late Henry L. Dougherty who had owned the hotel before his demise, were assigned to the royal party. Again, I was sleeping almost up in the clouds. I remember being rather concerned that evening when a terrific thunderstorm struck the vicinity. The lightning flashed all around and the thunder bellowed. From my vantage point on the sheltered balcony outside of my bedroom, I watched nature at work, or play, for miles in every direction. I wondered how the Duchess was faring.

The next day I flew over to Nassau ahead of the royal party, who returned to the Bahamas via boat. A severe hurricane had struck New Providence during our prolonged absence and Nassau was in a very unsettled state, both politically and economically. I was happy to be back in order to catch my breath for a while and get a little well-earned rest after those full and strenuous travel days with the Duke and Duchess.

The Duchess of Windsor's Party, "New York at War".
Source: Author's collection.

THE MURDER OF SIR HARRY OAKES,
THE BAHAMAS' RICHEST MAN

His Royal Highness was a man of action. The ruthless murder of Sir Harry Oakes on 7 or 8 July 1943, was a heavy blow to the Governor. Sir Harry was his friend and Island advisor. I remember so vividly the urgent early-morning telephone call around 7 a.m. on 8 July, which announced to the Duke that Sir Harry's bludgeoned and burned body had been discovered earlier that day in the bedroom of his palatial seaside home at Westbourne. An attempt had been made to set the body and mansion on fire. I omit the ghastly details of the affair, but there was no doubt that it was murder and not suicide.

After speaking to the Chief of Police, Colonel Erskine Lindop, HRH summoned me to his private study and his face reflected his horror. He was utterly astounded by the circumstances surrounding the murder. He repeated, "I just can't believe it!"

Without wasting a moment and with the thought in mind to get experts on the case, the Duke had me put through a long distance call to Captain Melchen of the Miami Homicide Squad and requested him to board the first plane over to New Providence. Captain Eddie had always served the Duke and Duchess faithfully as their personal police liaison officer on trips to Florida and was a man who had investigated many a homicide in his time. Any insinuation that HRH muffed the investigation at the outset is erroneous. I was there and I know. Captain Eddie was on the first plane out of Miami (his papers had to be fixed-up later) and he reported for duty at the Governor's office by noon.

Sir Harry, a millionaire many times over, was the Island's "Santa" in the sense of giving the natives plenty of manual employment. He was certainly ruthless, but he was a man of experience. I used to see him off the highway on one or another of his vast real estate tracts, working harder than his native helpers. There he would be driving a huge tractor, personally conducting the clearing away of the brush. He would wave to me as I drove by. Sir Harry has been made out an autocratic tyrant. I judge him only as I knew him. He was always friendly to me, though a bit brusque, and completely democratic for all his enormous wealth.

I recall the occasion when Sir Harry was traveling over to Miami on the same ship, the *S.S. Berkshire*, which carried the Duke and Duchess and part of their staff on their first trip to Palm Beach. I was standing at the rail in company with Sir Harry. As we rounded the lighthouse, the ever-watchful guardian of the harbor of Nassau, Sir Harry called my attention to the huge shark on the surface with jaws wide open, just in the process of consuming an almost equally large fish! We had a pleasant chat together. Likewise, I always had a high regard for Lady Oakes, a very charming, motherly-type woman. She shared her husband's many Island interests, especially humanitarian work. Sir Harry and Lady Oakes were frequent guests at Government House dinner parties.

The trial of Sir Harry's son-in-law, Count Alfred de Marigny, accused of the murder and his subsequent acquittal, is now a matter of criminal history. Although I never met the Count personally, I saw him many times with his attractive wife, Nancy, at the Nassau Yacht Club where my husband and I were also members. Many years her senior, he had married Nancy a few days after she turned 18 in New York without the knowledge of her parents. My husband, however, knew him as well as his friend, the Count de Visdeloux, who supported him at the trial.

The attorney for the defense was the Hon. Godfrey Higgs. I knew him because Mrs. Higgs and I were co-volunteers at the Duchess's United Services Canteen. I also knew the Hon. Harold Christie, the mystery quantity in the whole affair. He was a guest at Sir Harry's home the night of the crime. Mr. Christie was a member of the Governor's Executive Council and we often had long conversations on business matters. As the leading real estate developer in Nassau at the time, he owned a great deal of prime developable land on the Island and counted on a resurgence of tourism and foreign investment to boost his fortunes after the war[28].

Through Captain Melchen, who was a good friend of mine, I had interesting chats with some of the leading investigators of the murder – Captain James Barker of the Miami Police Department and Mr. Frank Conway of the New York Police, Department of Identification. Mr. Raymond Schindler, the renowned special investigator who was called into the case by the defense and Mr. Earle Stanley Gardner, who covered the Oakes-de Marigny murder case for the *New York Journal American* were important figures on the scene.

Just prior to the trial, for obvious reasons, the Duke and Duchess decided to go on holiday to New York. So, of necessity, I was absent from Nassau and missed attending the trial sessions, which I heard from all sides were packed with excitement. After my return south, Captain Eddie Melchen's sidelights on the crime were amazingly revealing to me. But the case is closed, and his convictions about the case must be left unsaid.

---

[28] Harold Christie deepened his associations with the Windsors. On 6 February 1941, he gave them the first big party of the season and the first ever by a Bahamian for a Governor and his wife. Among the guests were (the Duchess's) Aunt Bessie, Sir Harry and Lady Oakes, Captain and Mrs. Vyvyan Drury and the (Axel) Wenner-Grens.

Michael Hardcastle-Taylor writes:

The murder of Sir Harry Oakes on 8 July 1943 in Nassau knocked details of World War II battles in Sicily, North Africa, the Soviet Union and the Pacific off the front pages of most of the English-speaking world's newspapers. A strange, sensational and ghastly crime had been committed against one of the world's richest men, who with his wife were among the most prominent citizens of the Bahamas and close personal friends of the Duke and Duchess of Windsor.

The Duke and Duchess had stayed in Sir Harry's home at Westbourne, now a crime scene, for an extended period just after their arrival in Nassau and during the renovation of Government House, which the Duchess directed and supervised. This crime quickly turned a relatively quiet tropical paradise into a magnet for newspaper and magazine reporters, as well as detectives and criminologists attracted to the mysterious crime and trial over the ensuing five or six months.

The author and other staff members who served at Government House during the crime and trial maintained an almost complete silence about these events at the time and remained equally silent about them in later life. The Duke and Duchess absented themselves to America during the trial and said essentially nothing about it later in their respective memoirs. The absence of speculation by these and other people closest to the victim is curious indeed. Nonetheless, because the author mentions and knew quite well many of the key players in the incredible trial that followed, a summary of the crime and trial follows along with the Duchess's own words:

The accused, (titular) Count Alfred de Marigny, was acquitted by a jury of his white peers, the investigation of the crime having been muddled by two American detectives. One, Captain Melchen, was actually invited to intervene from Miami by the Duke. Together with the labor riots and the Bay Street fire of 1942, this trial appears to have been a vexing problem for the Duke in an otherwise successful wartime governorship.

The words of the Duchess of Windsor regarding this crisis during her time in Nassau may be of interest to the reader in addition to the relatively few words that the author included about the crime in this memoir. Therefore, I have set off in quotes below relevant words from the Duchess's memoirs published in 1956. This memoir was likely known to and read by the author, and it is likely that the Duchess and the author had more than a few discussions about this terrible crime during its lengthy aftermath, as they both experienced what they knew about it together in Government House.

The Duchess of Windsor:

"By our third year in the Bahamas things had really begun to go smoothly, despite

the strains and stress of war and the serious dislocations of the economy of the colony. By this time too, we had many friends. Among the most interesting of these was a famous and wealthy mining magnate, Sir Harry Oakes, a native of the State of Maine, who had made a fabulous gold strike in Ontario some thirty years before. He later became a British subject and took up residence in Nassau, where he became active in the development of the island.

When David and I came to know him, he was in his middle sixties, a small but impressive man, with curly grey hair. In spite of his great affluence, he affected a scorn for the conventional niceties that normally go with his station; he still preferred the rough garb of a prospector, spurned neckties and coats, and liked nothing better than to take the controls of a bulldozer and level acres of palmetto trees in a series of furious rushes.

Lady Oakes, by contrast, was calm, dignified and gentle; she was a pretty woman, pale of complexion, with unusual green-blue eyes. We saw a good deal of them and often visited them at their home, Westbourne, where we had lived for a while during our first months in Nassau. David, who was always attracted to the pioneering type, was fascinated watching the progress of Sir Harry's clearing operations. The last time we saw him, only five days before his shocking murder, he was happily engaged in filling a swamp on the edge of his property with a bulldozer.

On the night of his murder, 8 July 1943, it was pouring rain. At seven o'clock the next morning David and I were awakened by a knocking on our door. David opened it and was astonished to find standing there Gray Phillips. Snatches of their conversation came to me – something about a murder. David came back to the room and told me what he had just heard – Harry Oakes had been murdered in his bed. I just couldn't believe it. It seemed incredible to me that anybody could so hate such a good man.

David immediately conferred with the Attorney-General and the Chief of Police. There were no clues as to the identity of the murderer; more serious still, the Bahamas police had no up-to-date detection equipment. Their finger-printing apparatus was inadequate. The need for the latter was crucial because in the high humidity of the island, fingerprints and other clues would be quickly obliterated by the dampness. It was obvious to David that chances of identifying the murderer would be all but lost in a matter of hours, unless an expert with the necessary equipment was brought in immediately. The nearest place with such resources was Miami.

During the course of his several visits there to confer with Admiral Kauffman, David had been assigned as a bodyguard Captain Edward Melchen of the Miami police, who had impressed him favorably. With the approval of his own officials, David telephoned

75

the Miami Police Department and asked to have Captain Melchen with the necessary assistants and equipment flown to Nassau immediately. This was done. Unfortunately, Melchen was unable to develop any fingerprints or run down any other clues of real value. The murder remains unsolved to this day. The sense of shock and horror sent through the colony by this crime and the mystery as to its perpetrator were never quite dispelled during the remaining time we were there."

Source: *The Heart Has Its Reasons, the Duchess of Windsor,* Michael Joseph Ltd., London, 1956, pp. 353-355.

Count Alfred de Marigny leaves the Nassau Central Police Station on the way to his trial. Source: Photo by Ralph Morse, Life Magazine, 22 November 1943, in the Author's collection.

Transformation of Government House

As already stated, the Duke and Duchess of Windsor were perfectionists. Beginning with the start of official duties in 1940 and continuing until early 1945, Government House was transformed and beautified, within and without, a monumental testimonial to the decorating and landscaping efforts of the royal couple. The Duke loved his gardening and was masterful at it. The Duchess, as President of the Nassau Garden Club, shared his interest. The Duke sketched out landscaping changes covering the 18 acres or so comprising the Government House property and worked out mass arrangements of royal poinciana, bougainvillea and hibiscus plants. He even took upon himself the re-planting of many massive palm trees.

Like his friend Sir Harry Oakes, the Duke worked as hard, if not more energetically, than his native helpers. The extensive rock garden contained manifold varieties of greenery and flowers which, together with a waterfall at the base, was an expert's task to design, construct and maintain. The construction of the goldfish ponds at the lower end of the formal gardens also reflected the Duke's creative artistry. The Duchess held her Red Cross fairs and garden parties for charity in this formal part of the garden.

Of course, the official head gardener was an expert too. During all this work though, I must admit, I was a trifle nervous at first in connection with some of the Duke's garden helpers who did most of the manual labor. They were Nassauvian native prisoners, who had progressed to being trusties and they arrived each morning in a truck under police escort. At the close of work late each afternoon, they would assemble and check in by roll call, only to be taken back to jail. No doubt the working conditions in the tropical breezes at Government House were better for these prisoners than being stuck in a crowded jail all day, especially during the hot and humid summers.

I cannot give full credit to the Duchess for the entire refashioning of the interior of Government House. A close friend of the Duchess, Mrs. Isabel Bradley, who had a winter residence in Nassau and maintained her own decorating shop in New York, did wonders to the place, at no slight cost. One of my first duties on the job was to type out the covering inventory of the alterations, new draperies, furniture et cetera, when the work was complete. Mrs. Bradley and I went into session, with plenty of night work, and the long, detailed task was at last finished. It was strenuous work and we emerged good friends.

The Duchess carried out many ideas of her own and was always adding pieces of interest to the decorating scheme, thereby transforming a completely official, rather cold and dated residence into a tropical mansion reflecting charm and taste. I am sure the Duchess could have been an important and successful interior designer if she had turned her talents to that profession. She delighted in re-sorting and re-arranging the furniture and ornaments. The housekeeper had to concentrate on the repeated shuffles to make sure that the housemaids, under her direction, returned all ornaments and appointments to their new positions after dusting and cleaning.

There were many royal photographs and knick-knacks at vantage points in the drawing room and library – pieces of tremendous interest and historical value. For example, the lovely formal photograph and paintings in these rooms, including one of Queen Mary, an informal one of Queen Victoria, and going back somewhat further in history, a splendid one of the Duke of Wellington.

In contrast to the formality of the drawing room, library and dining room, the Windsors' own suites were quite informal. A feature was the many favorite photographs of each other in their respective rooms and an assortment of these pictures accompanied them on their trips.

The Duchess's suite comprised four rooms – a bedroom, dressing room, verandah-study and bathroom, and was toned in Wallis-blue and white. The French Provençal style prevailed, coupled with the extensive use of mirror, here, there and all around. It was charming, tastefully decorated and had a great many closet areas. Everything looked and was expensive. In the very hottest weather, the dainty flowered French crêpe-de-chine sheets intrigued me. Otherwise, the linen in varied pastel tones was monogrammed impressively with a coronet.

In contrast, the Duke's suite, primarily decorated in bamboo, was sportingly masculine. Maps of the Bahamas and outlying island areas in bamboo frames were centered on the walls. Many of the Duke's cherished possessions were on display including his red velvet and gold Field Marshal's baton and a large red leather box marked THE KING engraved on the top in gold lettering. Each was packed away carefully and safely each night. The last two items were transported each morning down to the Duke's office by the valet and returned to their proper places after his duties were finished for the day.

Some items bore the monarch's coat of arms and some his own. A large, illuminated globe of the world sat on a nearby table for ready reference. The suite, more or less resembling a tropical club lounge, was very comfortable looking, a place in which to relax and to dictate and enjoy a cup of tea in the afternoon.

ANNUAL INSPECTION
by
The Duchess of Windsor
President of the Bahamas Red Cross Branch
of
2nd Bahamas Red Cross Detachment
and
DEMONSTRATION
—
Admit Bearer to Government House
—
THURSDAY, DECEMBER 18th, at 2.45

Name *Mrs Jean Drewes*

Entrance: West Gate

*The Duke and Duchess of Windsor made great use of Government House
in support of local charities and the war effort.*
Source: Author's collection

*Below on the left is the south (rear) side of Government House as seen from
the "Rock Garden". The Duke's Colonial Office is in the center and right.
The Duke used volunteer labor from the Nassau Central Police Station
(and jail) to develop this area of the grounds including a turtle pond
that remains to this day. The prisoners were said to agree that working in the
Duke's Rock Garden in the fresh air of the tropical breeze was far superior to
wiling one's time in the stale, rodent- and pest-infested jail. The annual Red
Cross Fair, started by the Duchess of Windsor in 1941 is still held on the
G.H. grounds down the hill and to the south of the area pictured.*

THE DUKE'S INSATIABLE CURIOSITY

One of the Duke's outstanding qualities was his curious interest in everything. As an executive, at home and at play, he simply had to satisfy that curiosity. The Duchess shared a certain amount of curiosity with her husband but not to such a marked degree.

On one occasion, the air-conditioning unit in my suite repeatedly failed to perform. It was a newly-marketed electrical fixture and, as the local electricians had failed to make the necessary adjustments, the services of an expert from Miami were required. The Duke took time off from his official duties to watch its dismemberment and re-assemblage and in addition, requested that I too should watch the procedure. Not being in the least mechanically minded and not having the slightest interest in what made the wheels in it go round other than having complete appreciation when the chilled air was emitted, I took the course. It seemed to me that the Duke was looking into the future in case something went wrong with it again, when perhaps he and I could jointly adjust it back to life!

On another occasion, HRH and the Duchess formally opened the Bahamian Industries Fair in aid of the Red Cross Fund. The Duke's curious and complete inspection of the immense turtle in the pool reached the point where he nearly lost his balance and fell into the water.

The Duke had a ready and affable smile when his curiosity got the best of him. One of the first days after my arrival, he picked up from my desk a shining steel ball bearing, given to me by a former employer of mine in a Swedish steel corporation. How the Duke admired that paper weight! He inspected it carefully and put it down. "Is that your very own?" he asked me. Slowly, I replied, "Yes, Your Royal Highness, my very own, and I have had it a long, long time … "

On my vanity I had an onyx trinket box with a jeweled knob. It was an attractive piece, also a gift. The Duke often glanced at that pretty onyx box as he paced up and down the room dictating some governmental or private matter. I would watch him look at it and then walk away and I thought as I watched him in between my shorthand outlines that someday he would be bound to look inside it. One day he did and he apologized for his curiosity. I smiled it off and my facial expression indicated, "Well, that's that. Now let us get on with the subject at hand!"

The Duchess derived a great deal of enjoyment out of opening packages. When the chauffeur delivered a collection of parcels to me that had just arrived on the Island via boat or plane from Miami, New York or some other distant point, I would just ask him to deposit them on the large mahogany table in my suite. I would allow them to rest there intact for I knew the Duchess would appear before too long and would enjoy supervising their opening. Sure enough, within a few moments after her arrival on the scene, a footman would be summoned, the parcels would be opened with speed, spread around, sorted and routed and the wrappings would be speedily cleared away by the attendant footman or footmen as required.

It was surprising how many gifts, especially for HRH, arrived at my desk from distant parts of the Empire. The gifts were from the Duke's former subjects who still thought of him as their own "Prince". Items such as knitted socks and initialed scarves arrived regularly. According to the Royal Family's procedure, all gifts from parties unknown to them were returned. Often there was no address given or the package arrived in such a battered condition from some faraway place, perhaps India or Africa, that the identification data was completely gone. I added such items to a box of miscellaneous collections for presentation to local bazaars in aid of the needy people of Nassau. I was amused sometimes by requests from collectors of various items. One sent me an empty vial to be filled with water from Paradise Beach, but I could hardly include the sunshine content of the tropical water!

New Providence populace turns out for Empire Day, Nassau, circa 1943. The Governor investigated and cared greatly about the poor living conditions of many of the Bahamian people, including those living on the Out Islands.

Bahamians turned out in large numbers for the parade and festivities on
Empire Day in Nassau, 1943.
Source: Author's collection

CLOTHING AND JEWELRY

Both the Duke and Duchess had a keen interest in clothes and were always conscious of the perfection of their attire for each occasion. At the cabaña and on his yacht, the Duke could relax in his favorite sports attire. He liked crêpe-soled shoes and all manner of jaunty sports gadgets. His shirts could never be copied exactly for they carried the embroidered coronet with his initial "E" above.

Since it was wartime, the Duke necessarily limited his orders for new clothes. In fact, he was attached to his assortment of excellent "old" effects. They were new old-ones, always pressed to perfection and ready for immediate wear, and although some bore date marks of quite a few years back, these were in top fashion because they were of a distinct pattern and faultlessly tailored. At formal dinner parties at Government House the Duke always wore a Scotch tartan. He had a full selection of these. For his outside dinner engagements, he wore a tuxedo – not the conventional black, but midnight blue. White tie and tails were not worn officially by anyone on the Island because it was wartime.

I was once called in to give my opinion of his Royal Navy uniform. Not having any such opinion, I was at a loss. It seemed the Duke had donned his Admiral of the Fleet's uniform for an official photograph with the Duchess. His new valet, not being an ex-Royal Navy man, was not sure of the right position for his epaulettes. I looked equally perplexed but helped solve the problem by locating some pictures of the Duke in naval uniform in his files. So presently, he appeared for the photograph, all the details correctly in place.

The Duke's interest in clothes extended beyond his own. Unlike the majority of American husbands, he was observant of the Duchess's choice of dress and was quick to note any new touches. One morning I smiled to myself when he commented upon entering the dressing room, "Oh, darling, you have your 'brownies' on this morning." I thought "Brownies? – what is he referring to?" I then spotted she was wearing brown slippers.

I am certain the Duke's interest in ladies' wear extended only to the Duchess. One evening I had the pleasure of dining at Government House with the Duke and Duchess and Major Phillips. Though an informal occasion, I was in evening gown. It was royal blue, perfectly plain, and featured a new kind of electric pleat in the long, sweeping skirt. Later, when I was taking leave of my host and hostess after an enjoyable evening in their company, and was about to ascend the stairway, the Duchess turned to her husband and commented, "David— isn't that a nice dress?" I know HRH had no interest in pleats, but he muttered "Oh, ah … yes, yes … indeed darling … "

83

The Duchess followed her own fashion formula. In the Bahamas, she was always feminine in her attire and ultra-fashionable to the last detail. She enjoyed wearing playsuits from her large assorted collection, at the cabaña and on the yacht. I never once saw the Duchess in slacks. However, one exception was an oriental sort of creation in Chinese red with an embroidered hooped jacket over an Asiatic-cut pair of trousers, which she liked to wear on *Gemini* when dining informally with her husband. She was not a keen sportswoman, although she liked to dress in sports fashion as the occasion demanded.

She played "at golf" but seemed to enjoy swimming much more. It always intrigued me the way the French maid pressed her dressmaker swim suits, before and after use. The pressing requirements were time consuming for her two maids. My monogrammed linen sheets were ironed daily. I recall one pair of lovely fine linen Parisienne sheets with an overall green leaf motif which literally used to dazzle me, but I slept soundly enough between them.

The Duchess always had her eyes open for novel ideas in dress as well as interior decoration. At one Government House cocktail party, I wore a unique daisy arrangement on a shell comb in my hair as a novelty which I had purchased when holidaying in New York. This attracted favorable comments from the assembled guests. The Duchess, in her friendly way, smiled her approval of my headgear and commented that I got ahead of her in featuring it. Once, for a belt on his gay blue doeskin slacks, the Duke made use of a piece of ordinary rope and unconsciously set a tropical style on the Island for the other socialites.

All my life it seems I have been giving people sales talks on this or that. Once, unconsciously, I gave the Duchess one such talk. For years, my family had shopped at B. Altman & Company on Fifth Avenue in New York, and I was a completely satisfied customer. There were many items needed at Government House, little miscellaneous things, which I knew Altman's could supply, as well as major ones. So I wrote an introductory letter to the firm with an order or two and received a prompt response to the effect that the items had all been located and were on their way to Nassau; furthermore, any future requests would be filled as soon as humanly possible, if not sooner. The letter was signed "Barbara Adams" for B. Altman & Co.

As the weeks went by, Barbara Adams and I carried on a voluminous correspondence and the service was beyond expectation. HRH would on occasion say to me, "Miss Drewes, will you please drop a line to Miss Adams and request that such and such an item be sent to me via air post?" And the Duchess would add, "I am sure Miss Adams will be able to locate that particular cooking item the chef desires … "

Later, being in the market for a fur cape, I wrote to my sister-in-law in Mount Vernon and asked her to look up Miss Adams, have her select a cape for me and forward it on to the British Embassy in Washington, where I would pick it up on arrival there en route to Canada. My sister-in-law attempted to carry out my instructions to the letter and failed to understand why twice, upon returning to the Fur Department, there was obvious embarrassment on the part of the staff over her insistence in meeting Miss Adams. She kept saying, "No, I only wish to speak to Miss Adams – no one else will do … "

After another short wait, a smiling gentleman with outstretched hand approached my sister-in-law and said meekly, "I would like to introduce myself to you, Miss Drewes – *I* am Miss Barbara Adams!" It was Milton Klein, Vice-President of the Company. He explained that he had considered the account of the Duchess of Windsor so special that he had been chosen to be my most efficient assistant all those months. On some special requests, he had worked together with another Vice-President, Mr. Keillor. They wanted the Duchess to be a satisfied customer at all costs. However, I blushed a bit more than a few times over some of my intimate descriptions of requested sports girdles and other items of feminine apparel which I had addressed to Miss Adams.

Later, through the medium of this prominent department store in New York, the Duchess also became a promoter for the introduction of coconut straw and sisal mats, ornaments of dyed fish scales and jewelry created out of shells into the New York market. These native creations, marketed under the Duchess's personal endorsement, were quickly popularized and greatly improved the revenue of the Island craftswomen.

HRH had a unique collection of jewelry. His jeweled evening cigarette cases were of novel design. The valet showed me one that depicted the map of Europe, giving in tracery form the various stopping points of some particular trip (Nice, Paris etc.) in precious jewels. I presume this was a gift from his wife. I recall a set of massive gold cuff links which had been presented to him years before by his cousin, the Kaiser. In British fashion, the Duke wore a signet ring on the little finger of his left hand, made of strips of silver, gold and platinum. He had matching sets of studs and cuff links, created of pearls, rubies, star sapphires, et cetera. Around his neck, there hung from a fine gold chain a number of jeweled trinkets – kingly and personal identifications.

The Duchess loved beautiful jewelry. I used to relish my contacts with the leading jewelers in New York and Palm Beach. When on occasion I made business calls to their respective shops, I enjoyed previews of fabulous collections of matching jewels in their private showrooms. Strangely enough, at first I just did not realize that the jewels the Duchess wore during the day were real, though the diamonds clearly were. I thought they were expensive costume pieces. It wasn't until I copied an insurance list for the attorney that I realized there was nothing "costume" about them.

Once, on a trip to New York when I left the Island earlier than the Windsors and had arranged to meet them later at the Waldorf Towers, the Duchess gave me an exquisite, massive ruby and gold ring to take up to the jeweler for a minor adjustment in size. "Just wear it up there," she said. So I wore it but worried about losing it the entire trip and was greatly relieved when it was safely on the repair desk at Cartier's.

In contrast to the Duke, the Duchess was much more generous. One afternoon she was gathering up some items to be sold at the Red Cross Fair scheduled to raise funds for the needy in London. I happened to be in her dressing room as she opened up one of her large leather jewel cases. Quite spontaneously, she handed me a valuable semi-precious pin. "Here, Miss Drewes, I would rather you have this than some stranger. I will make up the difference to the Fair Fund, in cash, on this item."

Another day she came into my suite with a stunning Mainbocher evening gown, a royal blue creation with a wide full skirt and a striped sequined jacket. She folded it over my arm and suggested it might fit me. It didn't and it never will, but it will always hang in a place of its own among my effects. Another of her gifts was a sweet chapeau created by Talbot of Paris, made entirely of wired, tiny white shells. She had worn this hat the day of their official arrival in the Bahamas. I am preserving it in the hope that each of my daughters in turn will wear it on their wedding days.

Observing the Windsor jewelry reminds me of an unpleasant experience I had when I was quite a newcomer to Nassau. While staying at Cumberland House before moving up to the hill, I became friendly with a Miss Skipworth, aunt of the famous British shipbuilder. She sweetly included me on her guest list for an afternoon party at the hotel where she too was staying. Although I arrived a trifle late, I met a number of the top society islanders and was not overly-impressed with one couple who were obviously top-flight British with their respective noses set high above the common level. They were evacuees from London and may have been finding it rather rough without much of their capital on account of the war.

As the party drew to a close, I was about to retire to my room when I heard a distressed series of gasps from the direction of the high, wood-gated entrance. So I casually strolled over to the area and found "Mrs. X" in a state of hysteria. Her ruby bracelet was broken and six jewels were apparently lost. She was in tears and announced that it had taken Cartier's in Paris six months to make the bracelet and now the rubies were missing. Considering the layout of the nearby gutter and drain, they did indeed seem gone.

Being a friendly American, I stepped up and asked if I could be of any service and said that I would be glad to try to find the jewels. I got down on my knees and combed the small grass area with my rather elongated fingernails and miraculously found every one of the six missing rubies. They were readily accepted and the tears disappeared. But I could never understand why the owner of those rubies did not have the courtesy to thank me. Perhaps I was simply "one of those foreigners" to her.

The Duchess was always handsomely bejeweled and immaculately groomed. Her gowns fitted her to within a quarter of an inch. One could not help but be fascinated by her presence. Her eyes had a searching quality, almost to the point of gazing through you. She carried herself with the dignity of her station and petite though she was, she was always impressive. Observing her closely reminded me of a similar impresson of real charm I had witnessed a few years before.

I had the honor of meeting Mr. Calvin Coolidge at the White House when I was on tour with our college glee club. Our fellow classmate and caroler, Miss Florence Trumbull, daughter of the Governor of Connecticut and then engaged to John Coolidge, arranged that the ninety glee-clubbers meet the President and Mrs. Coolidge. Never shall I forget Mrs. Coolidge's poise and graciousness and the picture she presented, gowned in a simple, blue-velvet afternoon dress with a single note of decoration – a pink rose attached by a diamond bar pin to her gown.

The glee clubbers remind me that HRH enjoyed singing as was apparent one Sunday morning at a special anniversary service at St. Andrew's Presbyterian Kirk. A new pastor was to be inducted and the Duke and Duchess received an invitation from the elderly Scottish pastor who was preaching his farewell sermon. At Christ Church Cathedral, the service was more formal and the Duke could not let himself go but this time the Duke sang with tremendous gusto. Afterwards, he mentioned to me that he had noted my presence and that he certainly liked to sing the old familiar church hymns. I do not recall ever hearing the Duchess sing. I do not believe she possessed any particular musical talent.

Once at Government House someone lost her breath on being introduced to the Duchess. A dress fitter had flown down from New York to Nassau for an important event. There was limited time to make some necessary alterations on a new gown. I stepped into the dressing room to announce the arrival of the young lady and the Duchess, completely picturesque in a lovely pale rose and lace negligee with sweeping skirt and train, was finishing her toilette. She looked beautiful. I ushered the young fitter into the dressing room, made the introduction and there was complete silence, no verbal response to the Duchess's greeting at all. The young lady was simply speechless!

I experienced a similar moment of embarrassment myself one time and my face turned crimson. When I first arrived in Nassau, the Duke and Duchess were temporarily residing at Sir Harry Oakes' palatial home out west. On this particular evening, the Duke was to make a special speech at a Red Cross affair. He had dictated a draft to me at tea time, had revised it and I had done a rush job typing it up. Sawyer drove me out to the Oakes's estate to deliver it in person.

While awaiting the Duke's arrival, Major Phillips, looking very handsome in evening clothes, conducted me into the drawing room and introduced me to Captain Alastair Mackintosh who had arrived that day from Palm Beach. It was very informal. I was invited to sit down and quickly joined the conversation. Suddenly, the Duchess entered the room, dressed in a beautiful white chiffon evening gown with matching diamond and sapphire jewels. I was entranced by this fairy-book vision and kept right on sitting, quite spellbound. A few seconds later, I came to and got to my feet, very embarrassed.

The Duke and Duchess of Windsor gifted fine clothing and jewelry...

but did not purchase much of it here.
Source: Author's collection

89

SPORTING ACTIVITIES

H is Royal Highness was a keen sportsman and spent his leisure moments golfing, fishing and yachting. The Duchess preferred to devote her time towards being an expert hostess. The Duke liked to keep fit and always allocated a certain portion of his day to some sort of sport. Although he had little time for sailing, he was a member of The Royal Nassau Sailing Club as well as The Nassau Yacht Club, and maintained a real interest in the Clubs' activities.

He was a more active member of the Bahamas Country Club; in fact, he was a daily golfer. He worked tenaciously and successfully to lower his handicap and was quite skilled at the game. He knew and played at the Country Club with many of America's finest golfers of the time, often to support his wartime charities. In March 1941, he and the Duchess organized a Benefit Match in support of the Bahamas Red Cross Fund that featured Bobby Jones and Tommy Armour vs. Walter Hagen and Gene Sarazen. This event was much enjoyed by many Bahamians and winter tourists from America and Canada.

Just before America's entry into the war, the Duke and Duchess also extended their patronage to a tennis match at The British Colonial Hotel, featuring the Misses Alice Marble and Mary Hardwick, and Donald Budge plus another male exhibition player who at the last moment substituted for William Tilden. This event drew a huge crowd, all in aid of the British Red Cross Fund. It was a splendid top-flight affair for tennis lovers. These outstanding tennis champions were later entertained at a Government House reception.

The Duke enjoyed surf fishing at the royal cabaña that was located out on the west coastline, a half hour's drive from Government House. There, the Duke and Duchess both enjoyed swimming. There were cooking facilities and the Duchess often whipped something up to please her husband's fancy. Otherwise, Chef Pinaudier would have his delectable creations transported down to the cabaña with the second chauffeur, Sawyer, in the little station wagon. Sometimes the Duke would hold private, informal meetings with members of his Executive Council at the cabaña. On many a Sunday afternoon, I would be summoned for dictation on some urgent matter and would arrive in my little Crosley number.

Paradise Beach offered excellent swimming facilities and it was always fun to go there in a glass-bottomed boat. It was located across the Harbor from the center of town past the exclusive Porcupine Club. At this famed Beach, I was poised to dive into the crystal-clear water from an elevated board on the float, which was moored about 75 feet from shore, when my eye caught the sleek outline of a six-foot barracuda circling just below. I was terrifically shocked and nearly lost my balance. I signaled to the lifeguard on shore and was promptly taken back in his rowboat. At the first opportunity, I reported the incident to the Duke and Duchess so they would be on guard themselves.

Their Royal Highnesses enjoyed occasional weekends on the water. While he served in the Bahamas, the Governor purchased and used a yacht named *Gemini*, which he had to maintain at some expense. He used it for business trips to the Out Islands on governmental inspection tours at regular intervals. I maintained a close liaison with the Norwegian skipper, Captain Neilson, and his expert Bahamian Mate, Henry, for I kept the yacht's records.

The Duke and Duchess took a great interest in the boat and delighted in fixing it up in unique nautical fashion. Anything in any American shop in the way of a yachting gadget which was brought to their attention usually found its way into the yacht's inventory. When I first arrived on the Island, I happened to have with me a few American paper clips of an unusual type. Those simple gadgets interested the Duke greatly, and I had to make a note at his request to secure a supply for him on my first trip to New York. Aboard *Gemini* the Windsors could relax and enjoy each other's company without having to be on display before guests or the general public. For them, boarding the yacht was also an escape from the intense mid-summer, semi-tropical heat.

It was extremely hot in Nassau although in the shade there was usually a breeze. I remember the heat-reducing idea used by one diminutive native boy while he sauntered along Bay Street. He was on his way home, barefoot of course, and wearing but a pair of tattered shorts. If he arrived there with what he started out with, he was lucky. For perched on his head, supported on both sides by his tiny uplifted hands, was a block of ice about half his size, melting rapidly but also cooling the little fellow at the same time. At least he was ice-conditioned en route home.

One of the many projects and events supported by
the Duke and Duchess of Windsor during the war years in Nassau.
Source: Author's collection

Under the Distinguished Patronage of

His Royal Highness The Governor
and
The Duchess of Windsor
who will personally attend

An Exhibition Tennis Match
In Aid of the British Red Cross

MISS ALICE MARBLE   MISS MARY HARDWICK
MR. WILLIAM T. TILDEN, II   MR. DONALD BUDGE

At The British Colonial Hotel
WEDNESDAY, FEB. 12TH, 1941.   2:30 P.M.   £1 - 5 - 0

More of the many projects and events supported by the Duke and Duchess of Windsor during the war years in Nassau. Source: Author's collection

The Management Committee of the
Nassau Yacht Club

request the pleasure of your company
at the Club House

for Cocktails and the Presentation of Prizes

for the past year by

The Duchess of Windsor

on Friday the 27th November, 1942

at 6 o'clock

CATERING AND CUISINE
AT GOVERNMENT HOUSE

The Duchess was a considerable authority on the theory of catering. In her private study, she possessed a formidable array of publications on this. For the benefit of the British War Relief Society, she assembled a collection of her favorite culinary recipes gathered from her time in the Far East, the southern United States and in England, France and the Bahamas. This little book – *Some Favorite Recipes of the Duchess of Windsor,* Charles Scribner's Sons, 1942 – with an introduction by Mrs. Eleanor Roosevelt, enjoyed a nice circulation and helped the Society with its proceeds.

Each evening, Chef Daniel Pinaudier would submit in his "book" suggested menus for the following day's luncheon and dinner. Before retiring, the Duchess would either initial the menus submitted as approved or add constructive suggestions in French as to a change in the variety or the addition of a certain dish which she happened to remember was a favorite of a particular expected dinner guest at Government House. The Duke and Duchess ate very lightly at luncheon but enjoyed a full course dinner in the evening.

Messr. Pinaudier was a renowned authority in the culinary arts and enjoyed fame and a fine reputation as a chef in European circles. He told me that he had been chef to M. Paderewski, the Polish pianist, composer and politician, and a favorite of concert audiences around the globe until his death in 1941.

Daniel Pinaudier had served the Duke and Duchess in France before the war. He liked to experiment with native ingredients. I once sampled them and often then asked for more. One was a concoction of chicken and rice with a delicious tropical sauce baked in a coconut shell, or rather a series of individual shells. Despite this rather crude description, it tasted so good. Although M. Pinaudier spoke English, I used to practice my sketchy French with him when discussing his tasty dishes. But with Marguerite, the French maid, I had to speak French to make myself understood. She was reluctant for some reason to learn to speak English.

M. Pinaudier used to shake his head at the highly-seasoned, odiferous native delicacies created by Laura, the Bahamian cook, and her assistants for the colored staff. An example was the popular peas, rice and onions plus fish affair, cooked Nassauvian style. Sometimes I would ask for a sample to be sent up with my dinner order. It was delicious, but in between mouthfuls I had to take a sip of water as it was so highly peppered. One of my duties was to keep the door leading up from the side section of the kitchen and staff dining rooms closed to exclude the onion odor from penetrating the upper hallway. That peas, rice and onions plus fish concoction's aroma was too much for the Duchess.

At Government House there were three cooking services. The chef catered only for the Duke and Duchess, Major Phillips, myself and Government House guests. Laura and her able assistants cooked for the "international staff" with Marshall, the butler, reigning at the head of the table. Another native cook catered for the Bahamian colored staff. Each morning Sawyer would drive the chef down to the open markets on Bay Street to make his selections and order future supplies. Special orders were flown in from Miami. A specially-designed charcoal burner outside the main kitchen aided the culinary efforts of the chef and his assistants.

I was in a dining class by myself and my meals were served in my suite. I would telephone my order to M. Pinaudier and within 15 minutes, a footman would arrive carrying a large silver tray, monogrammed with the royal coat of arms (for all I know it was from Buckingham Palace) bearing my special requests. I did not usually dine entirely alone for Detto, my faithful little canine friend, was very likely to be at my feet. Although he might have just been fed, he had a longing expression in his eye. He was on a one-meal-a-day diet and I was under implicit orders from the Duke not to weaken under the spell of Detto's ever-hungry look!

I know firsthand how good and genial a host HRH was for I had the pleasure of dining alone with him one evening at Government House shortly after my arrival in Nassau. The Duchess extended the invitation to me as she had accepted an invitation to dine at a charity event in which she and Major Phillips were both involved. HRH had elected to stay home. I asked the Duchess if I should dress for the occasion and she said it was not necessary as the Duke enjoyed being informal when the opportunity presented itself.

At 8:25 p.m., wearing a simple lace-trimmed crêpe afternoon dress, I appeared in the library in time to bid farewell to the Duchess, superbly gowned and bejeweled, and the Major in his striking Black Watch uniform. I admit I was a trifle flustered and distinctly flattered when a few moments later, in walked the Duke in full Scottish regalia, definitely dressed for the occasion of dining with me!

Well, we had a jolly good dinner. It was served on the terrace by Marshall and attended by the footmen, Gladstone and Johnston, with the little dogs taking it all in on the sidelines and wondering where their mistress happened to be. It was all informal in the midst of formality. I remember the Duke inquired how I liked the stone crabs which had arrived on the morning plane from Miami. I remarked that they were delicious. So, the butler was summoned and the Duke said, "Now don't be bashful, Miss Drewes. If you like them, have some more! I'll have some more too … " I did and he did.

We covered a lot of time and space that evening in our conversation. We discussed the crown jewels in detail and I told him how I had blinked at their lavish display in the Tower of London during a college-group trip to Europe. I was extremely interested in all that he had to say about the background and history of the larger gems. He smiled when I remarked that I had personally tested out the Whispering Gallery at St. Paul's Cathedral.

I still chuckle over the following question asked of me by the Duke. We had been discussing Oxford University which I had visited and out of a clear blue sky he asked me with a serious expression on his face, "Miss Drewes, in school did you ever win a prize of any sort?" I was rather taken back but must admit that I responded quickly, "Yes– three; a silver spoon for my spelling in the third grade, a five dollar gold piece upon graduating from high school and a silver pin for rapid typing at Katharine Gibbs School." He replied, "In my school days, I really tried to win a prize but never did … " On hearing that, I felt that I should have soft-pedaled my minor awards and let the query pass with, "Just a small silver spoon!"

I remember we spoke of the South of France, of Nice and the Cap D'Antibes, where he and his wife had resided before their evacuation and which I had visited on my tour of western and southern Europe. I told him of my brief visit to Monte Carlo. Although I was under admittance age (according to my passport which had to be presented), I talked myself into the casino and promptly forgot the ten francs that went to the house at the gambling table. The Duke was amused over my paying the colossal sum of three francs at the Musée Océanographique to have the garçon coax the octopus out of its lair!

We spoke of "The Royal Family" of the American stage and I commented that the Barrymores lived (at that time) in my hometown. How impressed I was at meeting Ethel Barrymore on one important occasion in my young school life. Her son, Sam, gave a party over at their home for his school friends. There was an orchestra and dancing.

We were allowed to circulate – in the billiard room and drawing room but not in the lovely-appointed music room which was roped off neatly as out of bounds. However, from the open doorway we admired the family photographs of Ethel, John, and Lionel as well as John Drew, their uncle, all impressively on display. About midnight, Miss Barrymore returned from her evening performance at the theater on Broadway and we were all introduced to her in turn. She was a regal figure and very beautiful. I remember she called out the numbers for the lucky number dance and though she spoke so softly, her voice carried all over the spacious room.

Another topic of conversation was horse racing in England, on the Continent and in the

Bahamas, which high society attended along with the native Nassauvians. The Bahamas ponies were as energetic as their native trainers. The Duke was interested to hear about the fine racehorses owned by my cousin, William Wallace (Tiny) Naylor, the well-known restaurateur of Beverly Hills, and how he had been the first owner to transport newly-purchased horses via airplane from the British Isles to America.

Toward the close of the dinner party, the Duke graphically described to me his descent into a mine while he was on a colonial tour of inspection on behalf of his father, King George V. At that time, he was the Prince of Wales and self-styled "Britain's First Salesman." The Duke commented, "You know, Miss Drewes, I have been a lot of places and seen a lot of things!" I agreed wholeheartedly that he certainly had. After that dinner occasion, he probably would have agreed that I had too.

The evening passed all too quickly. After rising from the dining table and chatting for a few moments with my host about this and that and the blanket of stars above us, I curtsied, gave my thanks for a most pleasant time and bade HRH good night.

I was most appreciative of the Duke and Duchess's kind hospitality when my brother and sister-in-law visited the Bahamas one weekend. They had met my closest relatives previously on one of our trips up to New York. The Duchess thoughtfully arranged an informal cocktail party at Government House in an endeavor to make them feel welcome. An engraved invitation with the royal crest and all the royal trimmings was delivered to them in top style by Sawyer, the uniformed chauffeur, over at Cumberland House where they were staying. The invited guests – Captain and Mrs. George Wood, Major Phillips, the Drewes' and myself – enjoyed a pleasant visit with the Duke and Duchess out on the terrace for well over an hour. The Duke was interested in Wallace's banking connection at the National City Bank in Wall Street, as petty cashier. I remember the Duke's remark which evoked a hearty laugh from all of us. He mentioned King Henry VIII. With a smile, he turned to the Major and inquired, "Gray, he was a relative of mine, wasn't he?"

I showed my family around Government House during the late afternoon on the day they arrived, at a time when the Windsors were both out. At length we landed up in the ballroom above the Duke's office and my brother could not resist sitting down at the grand piano and playing a few melodious chord combinations plus his "Kitten on the Keys" interpretation. He had been one of the first jazz piano soloists to play over Station WEAF in New York and once received a letter from a radio fan commenting, "To hear you play is enough to tickle the toes of an elephant and make him dance!"

On this particular afternoon, the Duke must have returned from his golf earlier than usual and he heard that tinkling music floating over from the direction of the ballroom.

He mentioned this to my brother later and told him that he too had been taught the piano as a child.

Later, Major Phillips joined my family for a famed Nassauvian turtle dinner served in the moonlight under the flickering lights of the electrically-decorated avocado pear tree at Cumberland House. We went on to the local cinema, and later to the Cocoanut Bar of the Prince George Hotel on Bay Street to toast the stars above. After that, we enjoyed the dancing of the internationally-famous Paul Meers at his cabaret. The Major would have liked to have come along, but as a lion of dignity in royal circles, the cabaret was "out of bounds" for him.

I had paid a previous visit to Paul Meers' place. While a guest at Cumberland House before taking up residence on the hill, I was introduced by Mrs. Jellico, the proprietress, to two newly-arrived guests from New York and their son. They suggested I accompany the latter to Paul Meers' cabaret, the well-known tourist spot, so we drove in a native fringed carriage over the hill to the nightclub. It was a dark night.

The club was crowded and eerie within. Paul Meers acted as host and chief entertainer, and a local jazz band effectively created the right musical atmosphere. "Mama don't want NO peas, NO rice ... " was the number repeatedly played for visiting tourists, most of whom were Americans. Meers' solo dances, as well as his duets with his French dancing partner, were impressive. He was a handsome charmer in his Nassauvian way – a Rudolph Valentino type. He presented a striking picture in his feather dance with his oiled, bronze body twirling this way and that on the wide area of the dance floor. The amusing part of this nightclub visit was that my escort happened to be studying surgery at Bellevue City Hospital in New York. He practically dissected Paul Meers, verbally, at every turn.

On another visit to the cabaret with my family, the place was dark and appeared to be closed. From nowhere it seemed, Paul Meers approached us from the shadows. He introduced himself and asked if we would wait inside the club for a few moments. He said he would be most happy to change into his dancing costume and put on a private exhibition. A while later he appeared in a casual dancing affair – black bell trousers, an open silk shirt with leg-o-mutton sleeves and with a wide scarlet sash binding his slim waist. He danced to the accompaniment of a local artist playing on a small, rather banged-up piano. He spun and twirled for our exclusive pleasure.

The Drewes family finally departed, leaving the nightclub behind in the shadows. Shortly afterwards America entered the war and tourists ceased to come to the Bahamas, so Paul and his partner left our beautiful Island to dance in nearby Cuba.

*The Duke and Duchess's French Chef, Daniel Pinaudier and
family with a Windsor dog outside author's beach cabaña, Nassau, circa 1941.*
Source: Author's collection

THOUGHTFUL, KIND AND SYMPATHETIC

A fter a few months of serving them, I came to appreciate that the Duke and Duchess were an understanding and sympathetic couple. One day I received a cable from California and was completely shocked to read of the sudden death of my father. In no time, the Duchess had Major Phillips enquiring about possible plane connections from Nassau and Miami to get me to the West Coast in time for the funeral. Sadly, however, the cable had come so late and there was no chance of my getting there. Realizing how I was feeling, the Duchess immediately invited me to join HRH, the Major and herself at dinner that evening at Government House and would not accept a refusal. All three were very kind to me.

The Duchess was similarly considerate to Joan Thomson, our housekeeper from the Shetland Isles, an efficient superintendent of Government House and a genuine person. She was a willing and frequent volunteer down at the Duchess's canteen. Many an egg she flipped to the order of servicemen. I always enjoyed my chats with her. She used to tell me tales of her earlier experiences serving in the homes of rich Americans, of the celebrities with whom she had come in contact, the idiosyncrasies of some of the houseguests and the antics of some of the well-known Hollywood movie stars.

Of all the cinema actors she had served, the one she liked best was Randolph Scott, best known for starring roles in western films. Unfortunately, Joan became seriously ill. The Duchess immediately arranged for her to have a consultation appointment in Baltimore at Johns Hopkins Hospital with her own personal physician and did all she possibly could for faithful Joan. We at Government House were all saddened to hear later of Joan's passing.

I met my future husband at a Royal Air Force dance. Somehow, our first conversation linked us together, perhaps because at heart we were very much alike. We talked of music and orchestrations, of our homelands and Nassau, and of the war. We found that we shared many interests and tastes in common and from the very outset, seemed to supplement each other. Presently I told the Duchess that we were very much in love, that Brian was my completely-devoted suitor, and that I felt certain he was the only one in the world to share my life with me. I shall never forget the Duchess's remark to me: "Miss Drewes, right here in Government House, you have no better example of unparalleled devotion!" That statement summed up the Windsors' romance.

Aware that many wartime romances blossomed in the Bahamas, the Duchess then asked me, "Was it the Nassau moon, Miss Drewes?" The Duchess checked out my future husband. I had casually mentioned to her that his godfather was Sir William Prescott, Bart., O.B.E., The following morning the Duke asked me for the exact name, as apparently he had looked up the wrong Prescott in Burke's Peerage. I told him that my fiancé's uncle was Frederick Brice, Manager of Bailey's Hotel, a well-known hotel in South Kensington. Uncle Frederick spoke five languages fluently and had acted as host to scores of foreign dignitaries. Another uncle had been managing editor of *The Lynn News*. The Duke was duly impressed and seemed satisfied.

As the wedding approached, the Duchess guided me through the planning of the ceremony, becoming my chief consultant. We had a wonderful wedding. My good friend, Mrs. George Wood, who incidentally had been born an Austrian countess, had suggested that the reception be held in the garden of her Island home, but the Duchess insisted that it be held at Government House. So, HRH formally loaned me Government House for the reception and an advance notice had to be reported in the local Nassauvian press (using specifically the word "loaned") as Government House was an official residence and I was not an official.

The Duke, as Governor, signed the special marriage license which measures over 12 inches in width by 17 inches in height with my name, Jean Drewes, spinster, on it. Major Phillips arranged the interview we had with the Anglican Bishop of Nassau to secure his permission to hold the ceremony at the Christ Church Cathedral and to obtain his special blessing.

The marriage was set for 5:00 p.m. on New Year's Eve, 1943. The Duchess helped me compose the informal reception invitations, worded exactly right according to royal usage. The guests, 25 in number, all had to have the couple's stamp of approval. I had brought my wedding gown from New York – a long, white silk jersey dress with gold-appliqued motif on the sleeves, gold slippers, long white kid gloves and a matching white silk jersey hat with shoulder-length wedding veil.

The local florist insisted on presenting me with a spray of Eucharist lilies, with white ribbon streamers as a gift to be inserted in a white prayer book. I was all set, even to the touch of blue belonging to the Duchess to tuck in my wedding gown for luck.

All seemed set but there was one huge crisis. As it was to be an evening wedding, my husband-to-be was planning to wear evening trousers, a white doeskin evening jacket and dress shirt, all of which he had acquired at the Men's Shop on Bay Street. However, the Duke thought otherwise. On the very morning of the wedding, the telephone rang in my room and his booming voice explained that at a dinner party the night before, he had been discussing the wedding with Group Captain R. C. Field of the R.A.F. Station on the

Island, and that they had decided that Brian was to be married in uniform!

I fear I exploded, that one and only time, in a mild sort of way. I got excited and said "REALLY, Your Royal Highness, you don't understand!" What he didn't understand was that Brian's dress uniform was rolled up in his kit bag. Fortunately, the Duke's valet Mears came to the rescue and pressed the uniform. Brian had his hair cut, but not too short, and he kept a vigilant eye on his best man, Eric Mills, R.A.F., formerly of the London Stock Exchange, to make sure he did not fortify himself too much down at the club.

Major Phillips gave me away, and so drove me to the Cathedral himself. We arrived on time, but as the Major said, "What's the hurry? The ceremony can't start until we get there." At last we arrived and the organ began the familiar tones of the Wedding March. Down the aisle, on the front right, I spotted the Duke turning to see if I had arrived. The marriage ceremony passed off to perfection. The click of Erik's heels, as he turned after presenting the ring, resounded throughout the Cathedral. Later, the Duke and Duchess signed the Register as our witnesses. Again, the Wedding March was played.

Returning to Government House after the ceremony, my husband and I were greeted by our guests out on the colorful flower-lined terrace. Marshall and the footmen passed around champagne and HRH personally toasted our health and happiness. My husband responded to the toast in measured words of true appreciation. Monsieur Pinaudier had excelled himself in creating a beautifully decorated, tiered wedding cake. Marshall kept the champagne glasses filled and the footmen were busy passing round trays of intricately constructed hors d'oeuvres – genuine masterpieces. The Duchess remarked that she had never seen Marshall so animated.

Everyone had a good time. Stanley Toogood, the excellent local photographer snapped his superb photographs. Brian and I made the rounds of the Government House staff, and called in at the kitchen to receive best wishes. It was altogether a dignified occasion, lightened by the Major hanging one of his bedroom slippers on the rear of Captain Moxley's car in which we left. Of course, no rice was thrown but as we were driving away, our friend, Father Holmes, a young Anglican priest, waved at the car and said, "There is some spiritual rice!"

We were guests of the Moxleys. Greta Moxley was Captain Drury's secretary and my assistant. We enjoyed a superb dinner at Cumberland House, sitting out under those magical stars and colored lights. Then we attended the New Year's Eve dance at the Nassau Yacht Club. *The Wedding March* was again played in our honor. We danced the New Year in. The whole wedding party stayed under one roof at the lovely beachside home of the Moxleys, and the best man, being lonesome, stayed on for the weekend.

We moved into a comfortable apartment at the Rozelda Hotel. We added to our number "Miss Hardcastle" – a striped kitty. Out at the Base, she had sought shelter from the rain and, feeling sorry for her, my husband brought her home. She had a wild streak in her and was completely unpredictable. When the Bishop of Nassau came to dinner, she insisted on jumping into his lap.

My husband continued his duties at Windsor Field and I continued my full program up on the hill. On weekends, we relaxed at the Nassau Yacht Club and enjoyed the bathing facilities and the dances. The Rozelda was next to the Royal Victoria Hotel. Before the war, my husband had had his own band in London as a side hobby to holding a post as accountant-auditor at the Metropolitan Water Board. He was an expert drummer with a very sensitive, strict rhythm. In Nassau, he formed the Windsor Field R.A.F. dance band which held forth on the sidelines of the dance floor, completely ceilinged with lofty branches of palms. We had a code. When the band played a certain number at a certain time and the tune was coming through the palm trees in the moonlight and under the stars, I would stand on the balcony of The Rozelda and hear the message "I love you … "

My duty-crowded days and the star-studded nights rolled by on schedule, as they have a habit of doing, and in time it became apparent that a great and most wonderful experience – motherhood – lay ahead for me. I realized that my days at Government House were numbered.

BAHAMAS

No. 428/1943.

SPECIAL MARRIAGE LICENCE

By His Royal Highness, The Duke of Windsor, *Knight of the Most Noble Order of the Garter, Knight of The Most Ancient and Most Noble Order of the Thistle, Knight of The Most Illustrious Order of Saint Patrick, upon whom has been conferred the Decoration of the Military Cross, etc., Governor and Commander-in-Chief in and over the Bahama Islands.*

To all to whom These Presents may come, Greeting:

(1) Here insert name, surname, condition, calling, and place of residence of Bridegroom.

These are to Licence and permit you to solemnize a Marriage between (1)

Brian William Wardcastle-Taylor, Bachelor, R.A.F. Signals Section, New Providence.

(2) Here insert the like information as to the Bride.

and (2) Jean Drewes, Spinster, Private Secretary, Government House, New Providence.

according to the provisions of The Marriage Act, you knowing no lawful impediment

to the contrary.

Passed the Office of the Registrar General

Registrar General.

Given under my hand and seal, at Government House, Nassau, this Twenty-ninth

day of .... December .... *19*43.

Edward

Governor and Commander-in-Chief.

NOTE—This Licence will be void if the marriage is not Solemnized within 3 months from date hereof. (Section 22).

I authorise the Very Rev: A.R.marshall to solemnize in Church the marriage of the above named persons.

Kenneth Churchill, Vicar General.

Brian and Jean Hardcastle-Taylor at their wedding reception at Government House, December 31, 1943.
Photo by Stanley Toogood, Nassau

REFLECTIONS AND IMPRESSIONS
OF HRH, THE DUKE OF WINDSOR

W
ho knows what was in the mind of the Duke of Windsor when he left the shore of his beloved homeland at the end of that tumultuous day back in 1936? I had the opportunity to observe His Royal Highness once when he was deep in thought. He was standing by the open window of his study with left hand poised on his hip and right fingers entwined about his favorite pipe, puffing away contemplatively. He looked beyond the blue Nassauvian sea far out into the distance, quite oblivious that I was awaiting his next phrase of dictation. In such repose, his expression had a weighted look, the look of a man who had weathered a great personal conflict.

I always felt that it took extraordinary stamina and fortitude to endure the political cruelties he experienced in his homeland. Yet, when his shifting glance caught the reassuring smile of his Duchess gazing at him from the large leather frame on his desk, his facial expression changed and took on the look of quietude – the look of a man who in his own mind, had solved a tremendous problem within himself.

The Duke adored his wife. There was no doubt about that. Although he was secretive in any number of ways – he was forever locking and unlocking private cases and metal trunks harboring private documents and personal papers – he was never secretive about his adoration of his Duchess. She came first in his life and he always tried consistently and continually to please her. Returning from the golf links of an afternoon, as he came bounding up the long, spiral staircase, sometimes two or three steps at a time, he would be calling, "Wallis darling, where are you?" Between them, it was "Wallis" and "David" – or as the Duke pronounced it, "dahling".

I smile now remembering the occasion when I stopped quite suddenly just outside the door of the Duke's study. He must have heard my approaching footsteps for he called out, his voice so full of anticipation, "Oh, Wallis, is that YOU?" Realizing what his disappointment would be, I replied meekly, "No, Your Royal Highness, it is only me with a draft."

The Duke was in the habit of checking with me on the telephone concerning the whereabouts of the Duchess and the time of her expected return home. When thus posted on her arrival, he would dash over from his office to hear for himself if she had had a tiring session down at the Red Cross Centre or at the United Services Canteen. He would ask if she wished to join him in whatever he had scheduled for the afternoon – a game of golf or perhaps a swim later. I always felt that just to be with his wife, in her pleasant and stimulating company, was all he desired.

Yet at such a distant point from his homeland, the Duke had strong family ties and he was always greatly concerned about the safety of his family back in England. He had such a worried expression on his face when he reviewed the decoded messages from London revealing air raid damage over the city. He was especially devoted to his mother, Queen Mary, whom in my presence he called "Mama" with the accent on the second syllable. Now and then a cable signed simply "M" would arrive for him. Likewise, he was always in touch with The King, his younger brother. In writing to him, the Duke used to dictate to me portions of his occasional personal letters and fill in the blank sections in his own handwriting; i.e., the extra personal parts. He addressed his brother as "Bertie".

I recall how crushed the Duke and Duchess were over the tragic and untimely death of his brother, George, Duke of Kent, in August 1942.[29] It was very late one night when a phone call informed me that an urgent cable had arrived from London down at the cable office for HRH. Shortly afterwards, the secret decoded message was delivered by special messenger to Government House and I called the Duke to announce its arrival. A few moments later, I was summoned to his study. There I witnessed the sorrow of both the Duke and his Duchess. The Duke was so shaken that it was an arduous task for him to compose the necessary cables of condolence to his family expressing his deep feelings.

I remember clearly when, in conversation, the Duke mentioned how close he and his brother had always been. As his older brother, the Duke had felt an added responsibility for the Duke of Kent's wellbeing. The entire household staff of Government House attended the Divine Service held at Christ Church Cathedral on 29 August 1942 in memory of the Duke of Kent. Likewise, the Duke had been saddened by the death of his great-uncle, the Duke of Connaught[30] earlier that year. A similar memorial service had been held in the Cathedral.

Early on the morning of HRH's 50th birthday, I shook hands with him. I was gratified that the Duke seemed pleased at my informality in saying quite cheerily and in friendly American style because of the occasion, "Happy Birthday, Your Royal Highness!" He smiled and quickly responded, "Why, thank you very much, Miss Drewes. Fancy, I have turned the half century mark!"

Here before me was a man in the very prime of life, a man in sharp contrast to the more youthful and carefree Prince of Wales I had gazed at so admiringly before the

---

[29] HRH The Prince George, Duke of Kent (1902-42), the Duke's younger brother, was killed in an air accident on 25 August 1942.

[30] HRH The Prince Arthur, Duke of Connaught (1850-1942), Queen Victoria's favourite son.

gates of Buckingham Palace a few years back when he rode past in an open carriage in company with King Fuad of Egypt. Here was a man who reflected his deep concern over the crises that were popping up all over the world horizon. Here was a man who was separated from the scenes of wartime action. Here was a man who already had lived a full life in comparison with others, a man who had enjoyed all the finest advantages that could possibly be offered an individual, a man trained and geared to do an executive job, in a big capacity.

Was he frustrated? Of course, he was. The executive control of an island domain numbering a few hundred cays was hardly an adequate substitute for one who had been King and ruler of the British Empire and now was HRH The Duke of Windsor, K.G., K.T., K.P., et cetera, Governor and Commander-in-Chief In and Over the Bahama Islands. Yet I felt in a measure that he had a sense of satisfaction and a sense of happiness. At least, he felt he had a job and was serving his country, even though in a role as small as it was. I admired him for his willingness to accept that role to the fullest of his ability and energy.

The Duke and Duchess of Windsor at either a "National Day of Prayer by the Desire of HM The King" or a Memorial Service for his younger brother HRH The Prince George, Duke of Kent. Prince George died in a Royal Air Force flying accident in Scotland in 1942. The Duke and Duchess attended the latter service at Christ Church Cathedral, Nassau, together with their entire staff.

Source: Author's collection

REFLECTIONS AND IMPRESSIONS
OF THE DUCHESS OF WINDSOR

At the time of the abdication in 1936, I remarked to a close friend, "I wish I had the opportunity of meeting Wallis Warfield Simpson personally, to be able to judge her at face value." I had that opportunity and far more – and the chance to appreciate knowing her. As our association grew, I felt she was my friend. I say unreservedly that I consider the Duchess a truly unusual and remarkable woman.

On one occasion, I recall the Duchess strongly intimated to me that some of her husband's countrymen feared his vitality and aliveness. Thus, of necessity, life for them was as it was, on the sidelines. I always felt that they were waiting with earnest hope for their chance to take a more active and important place in the affairs of the world. In their Bahamian roles, there was sort of a lonesomeness about the couple – a lonesomeness they shared, and because of it, I felt that there was a selfishness in their devotion to each other. Although they had a tremendously wide circle of friends, only a very few, time-tested over the years, enjoyed an intimate association with them.

The strongest link between the Duchess and her husband, apart from their devotion, was their mutual respect for each other's ability. Clearly, the Duchess admired the Duke's mental abilities, his salesmanship skills and dynamic qualities of leadership. The Duke, in turn, admired his wife for her brilliance and forcefulness. There was a quality of indomitability about her. He reverberated to her strength of purpose and between them there was a blending of strength.

The Duchess of Windsor that I knew was a devoted wife to her husband and succeeded admirably in making him happy. His interests were her interests in the Bahamas and elsewhere. I shall never forget in one instance her remarking to me, upon passing in the upper hallway at Government House, "Miss Drewes, will you remind me to remind His Royal Highness that his mother's birthday will be coming up next week and he will wish to send his cable?" That comment never fails to make me realize that although the Duchess suffered the deep embarrassment of non-acceptance by the Royal Family, she overlooked that hurtful fact in her effort to be a helpmate to her husband.

The Duchess was good company – sparkling company when she chose to be – and her hearty laugh was infectious. She had a keen sense of humor. On one occasion, she asked me to address a letter to a skin specialist she had consulted years before in New York. She commented, "I don't know what my name was then – perhaps he'll remember me!"

110

Another time, she was a would-be matchmaker. I was asked to dine with the Duke and Duchess and the subject of my being single became a subject of discussion. I chuckled and said that I was far too busy for romance – I just had too many other interests. My royal hosts and the Major were amused when I related how I had been a member of "The Unclaimed Treasures," a contract bridge club composed of four secretaries and four school-teachers representing Smith, Vassar, Wellesley and Mount Holyoke.

One by one, my friends had been claimed – except ME. I let the subject rest at that point. But later on, en route to the local cinema, riding along between the Duke and Duchess in the rear seat of their limousine, I was cautioned by the Duchess, "Never marry a man, Miss Drewes, with the idea of changing him!" I absorbed that bit of advice for future reference.

The Duchess had a way of drawing her husband out of himself. However, even when I was in their company in these private, informal and relaxed moments, I could never completely relax because I was ever mindful that the Duke was Royalty with a great big capital "R"! The Duchess was not demonstrative like her husband but it was always so obvious to me that when they were beyond the public's gaze, her devotion to him equaled his unswerving devotion to her.

During this period of their lives, the Duke and Duchess were sharply criticized by many. In my observation, they were understandably frustrated. Periodically, especially each time we traveled to America, there were rumors in the press of a marital rift between them. I used to witness their annoyance as well as their amusement over the reports and the usual denial always appeared in the papers.

HRH was even linked to the Axis in the press – a ludicrous claim since he always held in sanctity his loyalty and attachment to his homeland. It all developed because of his so-called tie-up with Axel Wenner-Gren, the Swedish multi-millionaire industrialist, who happened to be an Island neighbor. This gentleman was a very commanding figure, in height, in handsome features and in general appearance. At least I was impressed when I used to nod a good-morning to him when I happened to pass while he was awaiting an interview with the Duke. But indeed, Axel Wenner-Gren was an item of conjecture. There were rumors (after he left the Island for Mexico) that he had a loading zone on his widespread property beyond the limits of Paradise Beach for the refueling of enemy submarines.

Whatever Mr. Wenner-Gren's convictions and connections were was one thing. But the fact that the Duke and Duchess were linked to the enemy through their association with him was quite another. Because of the Duchess's dislike for air travel and the necessity for a tooth extraction over in Miami, the couple had accepted his kind offer of the use of his palatial yacht, Southern Cross, for the journey.

However, against all the barrages of criticism and rumors of affiliations and domestic unpleasantness, the Duke and Duchess of Windsor stood firmly together as a team. So these days (1965), regardless of rumors and implications about this royal couple, their devotion was a beautiful thing to witness and many a time in their presence, the words of Dr. Harry Emerson Fosdick came to my mind: "Not where I breathe but where I love, do I live … "

When at last the moment arrived which was to close the chapter on my Nassauvian sojourn and I stood in the presence of my royal employers to bid them farewell, a feeling of nostalgia pervaded me. I thought of the four years just passed in which I had enjoyed a liberal education in being so closely associated with these two exceptional, world-famous individuals, whom it had been my privilege and pleasure to serve to the best of my ability.

Even when filling their relatively minor roles in the broad expanse of the British Empire in a stellar way, the Duke and his wife had been untiring in their efforts to be helpmates in doing a creditable job as progressive leaders. They were in no sense merely glamorized puppets dangling in a social whirl but real hard workers and hard-playing individuals in an official post. I feel now, as I did at that moment, that they are a powerful team and it is regrettable that they have not been chosen to take the official place they deserve in this muddled world.

As I shook the hand of His Royal Highness and the Duchess of Windsor, in succession, and expressed my sincere appreciation of their interest and many kindnesses to me, to my husband, members of my family and my friends, it was with suppressed tears and a lingering smile that I made my last curtseys. A chapter of my life was finished. I went down the line, so to speak, of the English, French and Nassauvian staffs at Government House and thanked each one individually for the many services and kindnesses extended to me. They were all my friends.

At the airport, I bade farewell to my husband. I realized the future ahead was very uncertain for the Hardcastle-Taylors. We were depressed and we looked it. It was a guess where the Royal Air Force would next beckon or rather assign my husband. He prepared to return to the R.A.F. Station and await orders. As the door sealed behind me in the plane bound for Miami with all windows blackened for security reasons, I sobbed inwardly and outwardly. I admit that then and for some time afterwards, I felt a deep and abiding sadness.

The Duchess of Windsor at the Royal Air Force Cemetery, New Providence, where she laid the foundation stone during the Dedication Ceremony on Empire Day. HRH The Governor and the Lord Bishop of Nassau led the Dedication Ceremony.
Source: Author's collection

LAST THOUGHTS

Everyone is entitled to his or her own opinion about the Duke and Duchess of Windsor. I have always admired my former employers and readily join the many people in this world who hold the Duke and his wife in respect, and who resent repeated, unjust criticisms of their actions and worth. I have written in defense of this famous couple in the hope that my description of them as an official working team will evoke a more tolerant understanding and appreciation of them.

No one close to them in their daily living has ever covered the simple details behind the scenes at Government house, Nassau, Bahamas, and in their travels in America and Canada during World War II. I want you to know the Duke and Duchess of Windsor as I knew them. I knew each as a distinctive and unique personality and together as a charming couple, always so popular without effort and sharing an eager readiness to enjoy life not only through pleasure but constructive work.

Never in my close association with the Duke or Duchess were either of them unmindful of their duty or dignity. Nor were they ever second-rate performers. Knowing them as I did, I have always felt they were destined to meet and when they met, they knew their hearts were linked. That is my unshakeable conviction.

Now, as I type these last lines, I feel a little fatigued but still as focused as when I started out so many months ago to recount my four years with the Duke and Duchess of Windsor. Remembering my time with them in Nassau, as they worked together so well and devotedly as a team, has brought more than a few tears of joy to my cheeks. The tears flow from the fondness I feel as I recall the way they really were – to each other, and to me. Their humility and joy as a couple are depicted quite well I think in their Christmas card to our family this year from their home in Paris.

Jean D. Hardcastle-Taylor, 1965
Ben Lomond, Santa Cruz County, California

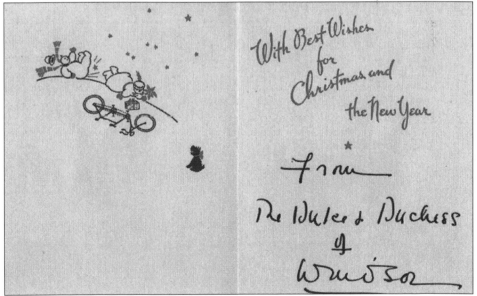

With Best Wishes
for
Christmas and
the New Year

*

From

The Duke & Duchess

of

Windsor

GOVERNMENT HOUSE
NASSAU

30th October,
1 9 4 4.

TO WHOM IT MAY CONCERN:

      This is to certify that Jean Hardcastle-Taylor has been in the Duchess of Windsor's and my employ as Secretary from December 1940 until July 1944, during which period she has carried out her duties faithfully and conscientiously. She is above the average at taking shorthand and her typing is excellent.

      The Duchess and I greatly regretted Mrs. Taylor's leaving our service for matrimonial reasons and I can strongly recommend her for any position of trust, and involving work of a confidential nature.

Edward

Duke of Windsor

Author at the time of her service in Government House.
Photo by Stanley Toogood, Nassau, 1942

Author Jean, husband Brian and wee Michael, England, 1945.

*A treasured gift from the Duke and Duchess celebrated the birth of our first child.
It crossed the Atlantic with the two of us in the convoy to England in 1945.*

AN ATLANTIC CONVOY AND WARTIME ENGLAND

Note to the Reader: What follows is a first-hand account about the conditions faced by the British public in their homeland during World War II. The Author's original words have been slightly abbreviated by her children.

L ife held no less excitement for me after I left the Duke and Duchess's employ. It has been far different to be sure, but nevertheless full of adventure, challenges and great joy. I returned to the United States and soon after, our first son, Michael, was born. Thoughtful as always, the Duchess sent me a treasured telegram while I was in the hospital bearing the message, "The Duke and I delighted to hear good news and hope both well." Shortly thereafter, a beautiful Cartier sterling silver porringer arrived bearing Edward's cipher (as King Edward VIII) on one side and inscribed, "From the Duke and Duchess of Windsor, August 29, 1944" on the other.

An important choice now had to be made whether to join my family in California or take passage to England to be nearer to my husband. I chose the latter and thus began another adventure—sailing across the Atlantic in a wartime convoy.

I started what proved to be a long process of packing right away and acquired quite a stock of baby supplies for the journey—those American traveling luxuries such as disposable diapers, tinned baby foods and Pablum. I assembled two metal trunks and five valises plus a wooden crate. My good-natured brother, Wallace, deposited me with baby Michael in my arms on the Hudson River dock. It was on a Friday afternoon in February, 1945, in the midst of a terrific blizzard. We kissed goodbye and he smilingly commented that, "All I ever do, it seems, is haul you and your belongings about. And every time you leave New York, it's snowing".

There was plenty of excitement on the dock. I heard among the crowd both British and Canadian accents. As it turned out, I was embarking in a ship carrying about 700 Canadian wives and children of R.A.F. men. For security reasons, the name of the ship had been obliterated everywhere so I never actually knew what ship carried us across the Atlantic. But I do know that we passed through submarine-infested waters with an air-plane carrier as added protection for our family ship. We endured twice-a-day fire drills and always wore or were prepared to don our life-preservers at a moment's notice.

The ship's purser, very British indeed, escorted me to our cabin and I discovered my roommate to be an attractive girl from Georgia with her year-old son. Already there was a line across the stateroom complete with drying diapers. I took the occasion to mention to the polite Purser that we could do with a little more heat. He replied, "You'll have to get used to a colder climate considering where you are headed, so you might as well start getting used to the colder, healthier climate here." I will never know how the four of us escaped developing pneumonia during that three-week voyage across the ocean.

Michael and I took it all in our stride. I found myself sitting on the left of the Captain at the first and only meal he took in the dining room during the long journey. He remained on duty in his quarters on the bridge during the entire trip and we enjoyed that Friday night meal. Our ship remained tied to the dock the entire weekend. As we cast off the lines on Monday morning and started to move away from the pier, I suddenly became very sad and went below to the cabin. I could not gaze a last time at the familiar skyline of Manhattan and certainly could not wave farewell to the Statue of Liberty.

The Chief Engineer was a jolly man and an interesting conversationalist at mealtime. Even he did not know just where we were headed. His orders changed daily and nobody but the Captain had knowledge of our position or route. I ate with my life preserver at my feet, and everywhere I went on deck and around the ship, the preserver was on my arm.

About two weeks out and as we apparently neared our destination, everyone was summoned on deck and the Captain stated from the bridge that we were approaching very treacherous waters. He informed us that there were a great many submarines in the area and that during the next two days we would all be on high alert. No one was to undress. As I looked around, I never had seen before (or since) such an array of ships. We were just a tiny part of a big convoy. The airplane carrier still trailed our family ship, and did so during the entire trip. The male passengers acted as volunteer lookouts for enemy U-boats. As we neared the Irish coast, it seemed that the convoy split into two sections. The major portion of the ships carrying troop reinforcements headed for the French coast. The remaining group, with ours as the flagship, turned north up the coast and entered the Irish Sea.

I and wee Michael arrived safely in Liverpool, England during a complete blackout. Moving slowly and cautiously we slipped into the harbor and dropped our anchor. We waited the entire weekend for our turn to start disembarkation alongside the dock. The docks in the area appeared ravaged by scattered bomb hits and the town looked totally dejected and war-torn. I felt a real pang of homesickness.

We disembarked in a lot of confusion at the very early hour of five a.m., with many touching reunions on that dock. The customs inspectors were everywhere but I was relieved of opening up all my belongings on the dock. During the trip I was concerned about the rather bulky wooden crate containing numerous breakables such as my typewriter, all of which had been packed professionally at a warehouse. I had left America with a conviction that I was going to make my home in England and my life's collections were now there on the dock. At least now I felt I would have them a little longer. Tea was served by the Red Cross on the train station platform and after consuming two cups, I was warmed up.

It was a tiring seven-hour train ride from Liverpool to London. The R.A.F. staff aboard the ship had assured and re-assured me that my husband's leave had all been arranged, that I had nothing to worry about and that he would be meeting me in London. Eventually the train pulled slowly into a gloomy terminal, which I believe was Victoria Station. I scanned the platforms up and down, on both sides of the train, but failed to see my husband's smiling face. It quickly became obvious that we were stranded. My luggage was on the platform, piled in a heap, and beside me was wee Michael sleeping peacefully in his little traveling basket.

At this point, I want to express my warmest regard and appreciation for the Women's Auxiliary of the British Red Cross. Not one, but a group of them, took me under their wing and transported me in a staff car to the King's Cross Station. Before I realized it, I found myself in a first-class train carriage with Michael in my arms, bound for the small town of Knebworth in Hertfordshire, about 25 miles north of London. Each of us now bore an identification tag. I was completely exhausted so I just looked out at the scenery, so green for winter, and wondered how long it would be before I could return to my homeland.

The mat of welcome was out for us wholeheartedly at my husband's mother's home in Knebworth. Through an oversight, my husband had not been notified of my expected arrival in London. Brian was now stationed with the Royal Army in Scotland, and after a hurried call to Scotland to announce our arrival, I waited 24 hours while he journeyed south. It was all rather complicated, but at least we were a happy and united family in England.

The next year passed well enough for us considering all the sacrifices being made on the Continent by the Allied forces and those of the British people we witnessed in England. But I was an oddity, and an American one at that. I just did not fit in well in the English countryside, which had practically no foreigners. I was the only American in our small town. I was lonely. Every now and then a shopkeeper with whom I traded would exchange a few words and return a smile.

The war was still raging all around us as it had been for over five years and life was very serious and dire for the British people. We were living within the radius of the flying bombs from the Continent. At night there was a complete blackout and overhead I heard the drone of R.A.F. squadrons going out for combat. It lasted an hour or so. Enemy bombs fell in the immediate neighborhood. The air raid warnings would sound at odd times night and day and I would pick up tiny Michael in the dead of night and huddle near the stairway until the all-clear signal would sound. In the distance I heard repeated explosions.

When my husband came home from Scotland on leave, we would sometimes travel down to London. There was scattered bomb destruction almost everywhere we looked. Westminster Abbey apparently did not suffer serious direct bombing. St. Paul's Cathedral, a top target, was hit in several places but escaped complete leveling. The direct hits in the surrounding area were numerous indeed. The people on the streets seemingly had reached a point where they were nonchalant about the air raids. The warnings wailed and ceased and life simply went on. From what I personally witnessed, I say very strongly that I have the highest esteem for the valor of the British people during the war.

In London there were queues for everything—to get on a tram, to enter a restaurant, to get a seat in a cinema, to enter the "underground". The movies were predominantly American and I always enjoyed surveying the posters announcing the coming to London screens of America's favorite stars—Bing Crosby, Betty Grable, Bob Hope or Joan Crawford. One always expected to queue at least an hour before admittance to a movie theatre. I saw many a picnic lunch consumed by people while "queuing".

Once or twice I journeyed to London on personal business at the American Embassy. I recall with amusement an occasion when I traveled in company with a group of typical "G. I. Joes". I entered the train at our village depot. Having become used to British decorum, I sat down and quietly stared out the window without really noticing the soldiers who practically surrounded me. I just couldn't keep a straight expression when one of the breezy sergeants exclaimed suddenly, "Say fellas, they're NYLON, why she's an American!" There we were, a half dozen G.I.'s from Brooklyn and the Bronx, so similar to the ones I had come to know down at the Duchess's canteen in Nassau, and me. It didn't take them long to tell me where they were stationed near Cambridge and what they thought of jolly England. We talked of home—Broadway, Coney Island, Jones Beach, baseball and so many other things. We enjoyed the hour's ride to King's Cross Station and upon our arrival, they escorted me en masse to the tram and wished me well. I felt homesick when I saw the American Army truck, with the large red stars thereon, awaiting them.

In December, 1945, our second son, Peter, arrived and Michael now had a brother and playmate. Brian left Scotland for army training in Oswestry, in the West Midlands near the Welsh border. One weekend I journeyed up there to visit him and had to stand in the train almost the whole way, at least six hours. That was how conditions were. Freight trains had precedence on the rails and passenger trains just had to wait.

From Oswestry, Brian received orders to Crown Hill Barracks in Plymouth, Devonshire. The war in the European theatre of operations had ended. We were all joyous that there were no more air raid warnings, but rather quietness and peace. It seemed only a matter of time until the war would be won.

We left the babies in a private nursing home near London until we could find a suitable accommodation near Plymouth. After a long train ride through the entire night, we arrived in Plymouth at seven in the morning. The town hardly looked like the "Riviera" of southern England. The bomb damage was appalling, a very distressing sight. As a shipping center and point of embarkation for the Continent, Plymouth had been a major target for Nazi bombing raids. Vast segments of the central section of the city were flattened. Schools and churches shared the same fate as the civic buildings. Here and there stood a lone sentinel. I wondered then too about the extent of the damage inflicted by the Allies on enemy territory.

We found a hotel and Brian reported to the barracks. I trailed around endlessly trying to find a rental accommodation. The following day I registered at the American Consulate and went to see His Honor, The Mayor of Plymouth. The Mayor listened to my tale of distress and personally assured me that an accommodation would have to be found, in view of the possible unfavorable publicity if word got around about an American woman with two babies (and her husband serving in the Royal Army) who couldn't find a home. Everyone, it seemed, was trying to fix us up.

It is difficult to describe adequately the desperate housing situation in Plymouth toward the end of the war. Imagine a derelict trolley car in an open field with no facilities whatsoever. It was offered to us at the fantastic weekly rent of the equivalent of $15.00. That was big money in 1945. The owner said that she would try to furnish it for us. The trolley car had two advantages—the roof did not leak and its windows were unbroken and could be raised for ventilation. But it was wintertime and there was no heat. We would have had to carry water from a faucet 25 yards away and cook over a kerosene stove. Amazingly, during the early years of the war under the terrible nightly bombardments, many Plymouth residents had actually set up tents in these same fields. The astounding part of the trolley car option is that even after our first glance at it from afar, Brian and I actually inspected it as a possible home for our family.

After several false starts, I contacted the classified advertising service of the local newspaper. Luckily, the woman I spoke with happened to enjoy visiting Americans and was impressed by the urgency of our situation and that I had already appealed to the Mayor and Chief of Police. Through their good offices, an arrangement was found quickly.

We had three landladies, sisters, in our new home. It was an interesting, rambling place, out of the city a bit and up near Crown Hill Barracks. It had been hit by a bomb early in the war and the glass in the front conservatory had been completely shattered. It was an older structure, to be sure, but it had a better-than-average bathroom with hot water. We occupied a bedroom on the second floor rear, and a living room with a dining area and makeshift kitchen up a short, steep stairway. A former Royal Army Captain and his wife occupied the front apartment on the second floor. We all got along very well; our landladies on the first floor and the two other families on the second. The Hardcastle-Taylors were happy to be there, in the back of the second floor and with access to the attic.

We had no heat in our bedroom and the hallways were cold. Our living room/ kitchen had a small, inadequate fireplace. We hauled our limited amount of coal up the stairs from the cellar. No coal—no heat! We rented a radio receiver, which provided programs from two stations and the collector came for his fee twice a month. I could have set my watch on his arrival at nine-thirty every other Monday morning. When the gas meter failed, it meant another shilling in the slot. No shilling—no gas!

I remember well the general conditions the British public dealt with toward the end of the war. Meat, bacon, butter, fat, milk; everything was closely rationed. On a certain day each week, I collected our family's rations at the different shops where we were registered. Each Saturday morning I called for my joint of beef from the corner butcher shop. The wrapping was newspaper. Vegetables were not rationed but scarce. There was no supply of fresh fruits to speak of and certainly no tinned varieties available. Fortunately, my family and friends in America were mindful of us and it was a great pleasure to open their food packages from home.

We had a very workable arrangement with our landladies, one of whom operated a taxi service from the home. During the day, I took telephone messages for the service or answered the door in their absence from the premises. My husband also did so on certain evenings. In return, they baby-sat for us when on occasion we went out for a little change of atmosphere. We especially liked to visit the seaside promenade named "The Hoe" and listen to the local Plymouth band. Every so often we would enjoy the high-class variety at the Plymouth Theatre and I remember one show that was extremely funny, "Soldiers in Skirts", put on by a traveling troupe.

I still fondly recall the excellent services of the children's free clinics throughout England. The babies did not go without supplies. Free orange juice (the concentrated Lend-Lease variety), cod liver oil and an English type of Pablum were rationed in adequate measure. Whenever the government received a shipment of oranges or bananas from somewhere outside the British Isles, the children and not the adults got their share according to the ration books. Highly qualified doctors gave the children periodic examinations. At the clinic in Plymouth where I was registered, the lady doctor became my friend.

British pubs played an important part in the social life of ordinary Englishmen and reflected class distinction practiced among their customers. Pub names were often very quaint—The Evening Star, The Roebuck, The Royal Arms, The Boar's Head and The Crown, with an occasional The Station Café!

At that time the pubs catered to three sets of customers and in some instances there was a fourth bar for ladies only. The Lounge, or private bar where prices were a penny a pint more, were for the "uppers" and those who aspired to be "uppers". The Saloon bar was where the white-collared office workers gathered to imbibe. Last, but not least in terms of numbers of customers, was the public bar for working class folk. The pubs were constructed in a triangle and divided into three or four sections as the case might be.

Most of the hotels and other bars were owned by the breweries and operated by private parties. In the villages the pubs opened at 10 a.m. and closed at 2 p.m., only to reopen at 6 p.m. and close on the dot for the day at 10 p.m. They were the natural meeting places for the villagers and groups to air their views on the war, politics, rationing, rising prices and Lend-Lease. A big topic of conversation was football and Brian and I would follow the Big League matches, and along with thousands of soccer fans, filled out our "weekly winner bets" in the hope of a huge payoff.

The supply of beer was limited. Most calls of the patrons were for "half and half" or a "pint of bitter". These were on draft and pumped up from huge kegs in the cold cellars, which needed no air conditioning. Popular American cocktails were unknown, which was just as well as the lack of necessary ingredients, especially ice, precluded them from being made to order. English pub operators served up wonderful Cornish pasties. In wartime they lacked a generous supply of meat; however, the small pieces of diced potato enfolded in crisp pie pastry never failed to delight my palate. Nothing could surpass a hot and delicious Cornish pasty with a glass of cold English ale!

Thus life continued as such for us in Plymouth. Finally, in October 1946, my husband received his demobilization papers from His Majesty's Service. Shortly after that his passport to enter the United States was issued. I had spent the entire year negotiating with the American Embassy in London to secure my own new passport with the youngsters included. At last, it came through and all was in order for our return to America.

Naturally we were counting on returning to America on the same ship but this was not to be. A red-tape foul-up with Brian's papers meant that he would have to take a later ship. After a weary two days of assembling ourselves for the long sea journey and a series of good-byes, the Hardcastle-Taylors boarded the early train for Southampton and stayed the night at a local hotel. Again, it was a sad parting. As we slowly moved off the dock, I waved farewell to my husband, not knowing when we would be reunited in America. I saw the last of Southampton, which like Plymouth, reflected heavy destruction from Nazi bombing blitzes.

Safely aboard the S.S. John Ericson, a former Swedish liner, it quickly became obvious that the voyage to come was best described as troop travel at an exorbitant price. We three were lodged in a crowded cabin with private bath, along with three ladies, two American and one French. A crib in the center section served as a sleeping section for my two boys. I must say that after such restricted food rationing in England, it was a joy to partake of American food once again. At our first meal all the adults ate until we could not eat any more. Each adult in our cabin added a couple of inches to our waistline by the time we docked in the Hudson River.

One of the ladies who shared our cabin became my close traveling companion throughout the trip. She was of invaluable help to me in the constant care of Peter and Michael. She too had had her war experiences. She was American and had been married to a retired British Army officer. They were living in France at the time of the Nazi onslaught and had just managed to get out of France on the last boat over to Spain. (Their escape mirrored that of the Duke and Duchess from Lisbon to the Bahamas just over six years before.) Virtually all of their personal effects were left behind. They took only what could be carried in a very small cart that wobbled drearily to the port of embarkation. Finally they had reached London safely and Alice served faithfully in the official Services' welfare work throughout the rest of the war.

We had our laughs, too, in between changing diapers and feeding ourselves and the youngsters. Aboard the ship was a large group of British brides of American G.I.s who had been stationed in various parts of the British Isles. With their own collection of lads and lassies they were also anxious to join their husbands in America. They were all placed in a section together and efforts were made to inform them about the basics of life in the United States. We heard some great war-bride tales from the ship's Head Nurse with whom we chatted to wile away the time on the nine-day crossing. I remember her tale of an English bride who was so excited about joining her husband on his "ranch" in Brooklyn. Another said her husband was a prosperous fur trader in northern Alabama when actually he was a skunk trapper.

Our French cabin companion was traveling to New York to be married to her G.I. officer fiance whom she had met in Paris. She had suffered grueling war experiences and had escaped death by slipping out of Paris to London when the German army took over. Her mother and younger sister had been seized by the Gestapo and she and her father had not had a word about them since. She spoke several languages fluently and was so enthused about starting life anew in New York.

The days passed very slowly but we finally could see the Manhattan skyline and the Statue of Liberty—a very welcome sight indeed. Unlike when Michael and I sailed from New York almost two years before, this was a sighting I would not have missed for anything. My heart rose at the sight of that imposing Statue at long range and I introduced my little Peter and Michael to her for the first time. A tear of thankfulness ran down my cheek as I now realized that we had returned to our homeland safely. And there on the dock, waving a special pass in his hand, stood my brother Wallace with a welcoming smile on his face and knowing expression which seemed to say, "Here I am, ready for the next hauling job!"

An irony of our passage to America was that my husband sailed on the next boat from the port of London. His was a Liberty Ship which carried only fourteen passengers supposedly headed for New York. He actually landed in Boston. So instead of having a normal dockside reunion in Manhattan, I welcomed him just as well on a train platform in Grand Central Station where my "unforgettable adventure" had begun six fascinating years before.

It was not long at all after my husband and I were reunited in New York that we decided to take our two boys and "go out west" and make our future in San Francisco near where my other brother Herbert had already relocated to work with relatives. We fell in love with the area and decided to stay on. Brian started work with the San Francisco Examiner, one of California's leading newspapers. Not long after, we welcomed our two daughters, Brianne and Beverly—now four children in five years— and ultimately moved 60 miles down the coast to Santa Cruz County. Our family has always been my first priority and focus so to help support it I pursued my California real estate license and my husband ultimately became the Real Estate Editor of the Examiner.

Twenty years have flown by since I left a wonderful life in Nassau and my duties with the Duke and Duchess of Windsor to be with my husband and start a family during the war. My duties with my family and professional pursuits have all added up to a big, wonderful full-time job with the proof visible each day in the faces of our four growing children.

So in closing, I hope that I have helped set the record straight about the Duke and Duchess of Windsor, at least insofar as they carried out their duties as Governor and First Lady of the Bahamas during World War II. This has been my goal from the outset of this long and stimulating project.

Jean D. Hardcastle-Taylor
Ben Lomond, Santa Cruz County, California
1965

ADDITIONAL PHOTOS AND MEMORABILIA OF THE AUTHOR'S TIME WITH THE WINDSORS

CHRIST CHURCH CATHEDRAL XMAS. 1943
NASSAU. BAHAMAS.

The author was married here on New Year's Eve, 1943.
The Duke and Duchess looked on from a front row seat.

The author enjoyed this beach scene west of Nassau adjacent to her cabaña provided by the Duke and Duchess for her personal use during her employment with them at Government House from 1940 to 1944.

Above: Author Jean Drewes relaxing with a friend at her cabaña west of Nassau at Cable Beach. Below: Boating in Nassau was basic in 1941. Just off Cable Beach, a few kilometers west of downtown Nassau, a Bahamian boatman rows, with Jean in the stern and a friend in the middle. Undeveloped Hog (now Paradise) Island is in the background.

When you took the ferry from Nassau to Hog Island you walked north across the middle of the island to get to "Paradise Beach". This is what you saw when you went ashore to begin your walk to the Atlantic surf at Paradise Beach in 1941. Below The author on Cable Beach as seen from inside her cabaña provided by the Duke and Duchess. The undeveloped western tip of what is now called Paradise Island is just visible in the background.

The author is seen here relaxing on the back patio of Government House. The ring on her left hand is a gift from the Duchess of Windsor and is described in her memoir at the end of the chapter entitled "Life at Government House".

This gold Cartier watch has an engraving on the case with a facsimile of the royal coronet and reads: "From WE XMAS 1941".

ISSUED FORTNIGHTLY

THE NORTH CARIBBEAN STAR

BY THE SERVICES FOR THE SERVICES

CORUBA
The Aristocrat of Rums
PERSONALLY
PREFERRED
BY THOSE
WHO KNOW
GOOD RUM

In the FRONT LINE of QUALITY
Zannaman's
Fine Confectionery
4 Arnold Road, Kingston, Jamaica

VOL. 2. NO. 9.　　FRIDAY, JULY 21, 1944　　PRICE: TWO PENCE

Special Bahamian Number

THIS is a special Bahamian number. We publish on other pages articles on different aspects of Service life there. His Royal Highness the Duke of Windsor, Governor of the Bahamas, has allowed the "Star" to publish the photograph of himself and the Duchess of Windsor which appears on this page, and has also sent the following message:-

"On the occasion of the special Bahamian Number of 'The North Caribbean Star', the Governor of the Bahama Islands and the Duchess of Windsor send greetings to all readers, Service and Civilian, and in particular to those members of the North Caribbean Force who are serving overseas with the First Caribbean Regiment."

Jamaica Meets The Army

The general public had a good close-up at the King's House Fair, of some of the types of weapons at present being used against the Axis on all fronts. Picture shows soldiers in charge explaining points.

This British military newspaper is the source of the cover photo of our memoir. It depicts the seriousness with which the Duke and Duchess approached their duties as Governor General and First Lady of the Bahamas during WWII quite well. The paper was published in Kingston, Jamaica at the British Military Caribbean Headquarters there. This copy was given to the author by the Duke and Duchess during her last weeks of service to them.

135

LIFE

THE WINDSOR TEAM

JUNE 9, 1941 10 CENTS
YEARLY SUBSCRIPTION $4.50

And this is what this memoir is all about. Finis!
Source: Author's collection.

136

About the Author

Jean Wallace Drewes was born in Mamaroneck, New York, November 10, 1907, the third of the three children of Louis Arthur Drewes and Jean Wallace. Her father was born in New York of German parents, and her mother was born in Scotland of French and north Irish lineage.

In June, 1928 Jean graduated from Mount Holyoke College in Massachusetts, where she majored in political science and comparative religion. The next year she completed the Special College Course at Katherine Gibbs School of Secretarial and Executive Training for Educated Women in New York.

Prior to her royal assignment in residence at Government House in the Bahamas, Jean had acquired extensive knowledge of music, art, and theatre, as well as international travel. During the summer of 1923, the author enjoyed a six-week educational and cultural trip through Europe, including a stop in England where she toured Windsor Castle and saw the well-guarded, lavish display of the Crown Jewels in the Tower of London. In London her group also attended a formal reception at the official residence of the American Ambassador. Her experiences while traveling throughout Europe often proved to be good background for conversation with the Duke and Duchess, and their many friends and guests.

Prior to joining the Windsors, she held several positions that led to her being considered for the position as their Private Secretary. She served as secretary to the manager of The Westchester County Biltmore Country Club, and as secretary to the traffic manager of a world-wide Swedish steel organization.

About 15 years after leaving the Duke and Duchess's employ, and having read a great deal of what she considered fiction about them, she wanted to "set the record straight" about their wartime service as Governor and First Lady of the Bahamas. She typed most of her memoir over the course of a few years beginning about 1959. At my college graduation in San Francisco in 1968, she asked me to help her with suggestions regarding the organization and presentation of the material. I promised her I would.

However during my Navy career I was able to visit her only a few times while on leave prior to her untimely death in 1970. So, over 40 years after she asked for my help, I began pulling together widely-dispersed photographs and other memorabilia my mother had collected during her years in the Bahamas. As far as is known, the author kept no diary but used her trove of Nassau memorabilia to guide her recollections and writing. Many of these, including unique photographs and invitations to social, sporting and charity events sponsored by the Duke and Duchess in support of the war effort or the Bahamian people, are included in the memoir. My hope is that they will make my mother's memoir an even richer description of the couple she served and the Bahamian people they served, and that, in a spirit of truth and loyalty, which were among her core values, she has succeeded in setting the record straight.

Michael Hardcastle-Taylor

Author's four children about 1956.
From left: Michael, Brianne, Beverly and Peter

ACKNOWLEDGMENTS

This memoir came to life following a Duke and Duchess of Windsor Society conference at the Hotel Del Coronado across the Bay from San Diego in October 2009. Fortunately, my wife, Gloria, spotted a newspaper notice about this conference the very day it started. We gathered the author's original typescript and a few of her treasures from her years in Nassau and headed for Coronado that same day.

First we met the City of Coronado's Director of Library Operations, Christian Esquevin, who recommended we proceed directly to the Hotel and try to find the organizer, Mark Gaulding, editor and publisher of the Society's journal. We found Mark, who immediately welcomed us to the conference (which we had effectively crashed). Fascinated with the idea that a rare, first-hand account of the couple actually existed, he not only invited me to speak that very evening, but inserted another presentation into his Sunday program.

Two hastily prepared presentations were well received, and I was encouraged to bring my mother's memoir to print. By the greatest of good fortune, we also met the conference's keynote speaker, eminent English biographer and royal historian, Hugo Vickers. Hugo also encouraged completion of this project and so work began. Hugo provided sage advice along the way, contributing his knowledge and masterful skills as editor. His contribution to the memoir cannot be overstated.

All this encouragement provided the spark and motivation to complete my mother's memoir. I started a long project of pulling together more of the widely-dispersed bits and pieces of her fascinating Nassau trove.

Shari Gallery, a friend for more than three decades, made the basic interior design something the author would be proud of. Her daughter, Tory, did the same for the cover designs. Her husband, fellow naval officer friend of 48 years, Phil Gallery, insisted I contact Michael Kastre, owner of Saint Michael's Press, who was of enormous help in getting our project polished into a published book.

My wife, Gloria, has been a stalwart provider of technical help all along the way from typing the original manuscript into a digitized document to completion. She and our friend Pat Hansen proofed and reproofed the final document with remarkable focus and attention to detail. More importantly, Gloria has been my principal advisor throughout the process, including reviewing literally hundreds of communications with the editor, Hugo Vickers, in England. The patience of Gloria and Hugo has been stellar.

Other friends, Roland Hansen, Nancy Padilla, and Shari Gallery, provided photographic skills to make dozens of 75-year old images more suitable for publication.

Finally, as we moved towards the launch of the memoir in Nassau, Hugo introduced us to Patty Roker, who was most encouraging in coordinating access for us to the Bahamas Archives, the Historical Society and Government House itself. What a wonderful 2016 visit this was – then more than 70 years after the author left the Windsors in The Bahamas—seeing the place where my mother's adventure began.

It can be said, rightly, that this project took far too long to reach fruition. To this I say, yes, but better late than never! I think the author, knowing her amazing patience and other skills as a mother and tutor, would entirely agree.

Michael Hardcastle-Taylor
Eldest son of the Author and Assembler of Her Memoir
April, 2018

SELECT BIBLIOGRAPHY

Blackwood, Caroline, *The Last of the Duchess: The Strange and Sinister Story of the Final Years of Wallis Simpson, Duchess of Windsor*, Vintage Books, New York, 2012.

Bloch, Michael,

The Duke of Windsor's War, Coward-McCann, New York, 1983.

Operation Willi, Weidenfeld & Nicolson, New York, 1984

The Secret File of the Duke of Windsor, Harper & Row Publishers, New York, 1988.

The Duchess of Windsor, St. Martin's Press, New York, 1997.

Bocca, Geoffrey, *The Woman Who Would Be Queen,* Rinehart & Company, New York, 1954.

Bryan III, J. & Murphy, Charles, *The Windsor Story*, Morrow & Company, New York, 1979.

Craton, Michael, *A History of the Bahamas,* Collins, London, 1962

Donaldson, Frances, *Edward VIII, A Biography of the Duke of Windsor*, J.B. Lippincott Company, New York, 1974.

Dupuch, Etienne, *Tribune Story,* Ernest Benn Limited, London, 1967.

Higham, Charles, T*he Duchess of Windsor – the Secret Life,* McGraw-Hill Book Company, New York, 1988.

Houts, Marshall, *King's X*, William Morrow & Company, New York, 1972.

Kinross, Lord, *The Windsor Years – The Life of Edward as Prince of Wales, King and Duke of Windsor,* Penguin Books, New York, 1967.

Martin, Ralph, *The Woman He Loved,* Simon and Schuster, New York, 1974.

Marigny, Alfred de, *A Conspiracy of Crowns*, Crown Publishers, New York, 1990.

Platt, Owen, *The Royal Governor... And the Duchess – The Duke and Duchess of Windsor in the Bahamas 1940-1945, iUniverse*, New York, 2003.

Pye, Michael, *King over the Water,* Holt, Rinehart and Winston, New York, 1981.

Vickers, Hugo*

The Private World of the Duke and Duchess of Windsor, Abbeville Press, London, 1996

Behind Closed Doors...The Tragic Untold Story of the Duchess of Windsor, Hutchinson, London, 2011.

Windsor, The Duchess of, *The Heart Has Its Reasons,* Michael Joseph, London, 1956.

Windsor, HRH The Duke of, *A King's Story,* G.P. Putnam's Sons, New York, 1947.

Ziegler, Philip, *King Edward VIII*, Alfred A. Knopf, New York, 1991.

*Hugo Vickers is an acknowledged expert on the Royal Family, appears regularly on television, and has lectured all over the world. His other books include *Gladys, Duchess of Marlborough*; *Cecil Beaton*; *Vivien Leigh*; *Loving Garbo*; *Alice, Princess Andrew of Greece;* and *Elizabeth, The Queen Mother*. His book, *The Kiss*, won the 1996 Stern Silver Pen for Non-fiction. Vickers' most recent work, *The Crown: Truth and Fiction: An Analysis of the Netflix Series THE CROWN,* brings his expertise to bear on that popular series.

Mr. Vickers is also Chairman of the Outdoor Trust, a project that inspires an active and connected family of 81 Commonwealth nations in the building of Walkways that provide interesting and healthy ways of seeing thoughtfully selected parts of these diverse nations.

Made in the
USA
Middletown, DE